SpringerBriefs in Psychology

Behavioral Criminology

Series Editor

Vincent B. Van Hasselt, Fort Lauderdale, FL, USA

For further volumes:
http://www.springer.com/series/10850

Brandy Bang · Paige L. Baker · Alexis Carpinteri
Vincent B. Van Hasselt

Commercial Sexual Exploitation of Children

 Springer

Brandy Bang
Paige L. Baker
Vincent B. Van Hasselt
Center for Psychological Studies
Nova Southeastern University
Fort Lauderdale, FL
USA

Alexis Carpinteri
Federal Bureau of Investigation
  Miami Division
Miami, FL
USA

ISSN 2194-1866 ISSN 2194-1874 (electronic)
ISBN 978-3-319-01877-5 ISBN 978-3-319-01878-2 (eBook)
DOI 10.1007/978-3-319-01878-2
Springer Cham Heidelberg New York Dordrecht London

Library of Congress Control Number: 2013948371

© The Author(s) 2014
This work is subject to copyright. All rights are reserved by the Publisher, whether the whole or part of the material is concerned, specifically the rights of translation, reprinting, reuse of illustrations, recitation, broadcasting, reproduction on microfilms or in any other physical way, and transmission or information storage and retrieval, electronic adaptation, computer software, or by similar or dissimilar methodology now known or hereafter developed. Exempted from this legal reservation are brief excerpts in connection with reviews or scholarly analysis or material supplied specifically for the purpose of being entered and executed on a computer system, for exclusive use by the purchaser of the work. Duplication of this publication or parts thereof is permitted only under the provisions of the Copyright Law of the Publisher's location, in its current version, and permission for use must always be obtained from Springer. Permissions for use may be obtained through RightsLink at the Copyright Clearance Center. Violations are liable to prosecution under the respective Copyright Law.
The use of general descriptive names, registered names, trademarks, service marks, etc. in this publication does not imply, even in the absence of a specific statement, that such names are exempt from the relevant protective laws and regulations and therefore free for general use.
While the advice and information in this book are believed to be true and accurate at the date of publication, neither the authors nor the editors nor the publisher can accept any legal responsibility for any errors or omissions that may be made. The publisher makes no warranty, express or implied, with respect to the material contained herein.

Printed on acid-free paper

Springer is part of Springer Science+Business Media (www.springer.com)

Contents

1	Introduction	1
2	Commercial Sexual Exploitation of Children	3
3	Victimology	5
	Domestic Victims	6
	Male Victims	7
	International Victims	8
4	Child Trafficking	11
	Offender Characteristics	12
	Mechanism of Child Trafficking	13
	Case Example 1: Sex Trafficking Risk Factors	14
5	Child Prostitution	17
	Offender Characteristics	18
	Mechanism of Forced Prostitution	19
	Case Example 2: Methods of Victimization by Child Prostitution	21
6	Pornography	25
	Offender Characteristics	25
	Mechanism of Pornography	28
	Case Example 3: Consumer, Trader, and Distributor of Child Pornography	30
	Case Example 4: Offender Networks	31
	BedBugz	32
	Trix	33
	Samson	33
	Redbed	34
7	Sex Tourism	35
	Offender Characteristics	36
	Mechanism of Sex Tourism	37

	Case Example 5: The Preferential Sexual Tourist	38
	Raul	38
	Case Example 6: The Repeat Tourist	39
	Richard	39
8	**Sex Traveler/Enticer**	41
	Offender Characteristics	42
	Mechanism of Sex Traveling	42
	Case Example 7: The Enticement/Grooming Process of a Traveler	43
	Case Example 8: Luring Behaviors of a Traveler	44
9	**CSEC Legislation**	47
	Legislative History	47
	Current Federal Laws Used to Prosecute CSEC Offenders	49
10	**Conclusion**	51
	References	53

Chapter 1
Introduction

Children are arguably the world's most vulnerable population. Cognitive immaturity, physiological weakness, and social naiveté leave children ill-equipped to survive in a world of corruption, coercion, and violence. Consequently, when children become the victims of exploitation, the social, economic, and personal consequences can be detrimental. One of the most poignant illustrations of this can be found in cases of trafficked and sexually exploited children. Researchers site the globalization of transport and labor markets as prime factors for the exploitation of marginalized people (Candappa 2003; Hughes 1999). In terms of child exploitation, this globalization, combined with high rates of poverty and the disenfranchisement of both American and foreign children, makes the commercial exploitation of youth nearly effortless.

The commercial exploitation of children is a global crisis (Rahman 2011; Svensson 2006). However, media outlets and sociological researchers have successfully situated the problem as a primarily Asian, South American, or Eastern European concern. In the process, the exploitation of children in the USA has largely been ignored. The continued trafficking of international youth into this country, coupled with the growing rate at which American-born children are targeted by interstate sex traffickers, speaks to the urgency with which the domestic exploitation of children must be addressed (Walker-Rodriguez and Hill 2011). In fact, research suggests that an average of 250,000 American children and adolescents are at risk of commercial exploitation each year (Estes and Weiner 2001). Further, there are indications that current data vastly underestimate the actual numbers of vulnerable and victimized youth (Chase and Statham 2005). According to the US Department of Justice (2007), no systematic efforts have been made to examine the commercial exploitation of children in this country. The low visibility of the crime, combined with the inherent vulnerability of the victims, have facilitated the continued victimization of these children. The purpose of this book is to provide a critical analysis of the domestic, commercial exploitation of children. A careful explanation of the differing forms of commercial exploitation of children, victim and offender characteristics, and the mechanisms which maintain the problem will assist health care providers, researchers, and law enforcement in their efforts with this marginalized and understudied population. We begin with a comprehensive review of extant literature in this area. Additionally, case studies of child sexual exploitation are included to further illustrate the severity, complexity, and depravity of commercial exploitation in real-life cases.

Chapter 2
Commercial Sexual Exploitation of Children

The most salient factor in the business of exploiting children is sexual exploitation. The pervasive and lascivious nature of child sexual exploitation has directed the focus of our work to the commercial sexual exploitation of children (CSEC). More specifically:

> It comprises sexual abuse by an adult and remuneration in cash or kind to the child or a third person or persons. The child is treated as a sexual object and as a commercial object. The commercial sexual exploitation of children constitutes a form of coercion and violence against children and amounts to forced labour and a contemporary form of slavery (First World Congress Against Commercial Sexual Exploitation of Children 1996, p. 1).

CSEC can more easily be understood as a form of commercialized child abuse; it is the sexual commodification of children's bodies for the purposes of monetary or material gain (Adelson 2008; Estes and Weiner 2001; Halter 2010; US Department of Justice 2007). The US Department of Justice (2007) defines CSEC as a three-tiered entity. It can occur on the local, regional, or international levels. First, exploitation can occur locally, managed by a single or small group of individuals with one or more victims. Regionally, multiple adults participate in the interstate or transnational trafficking and exploitation of multiple victims. And finally, larger national or international networks can support the organized exploitation of children. These larger networks of organized crime profit from the exploitation of children, procuring between $5 and $7 billion a year (Bump and Duncan 2003). An increasing number of exploiters, traffickers, and organized crime syndicates have become involved in the trade. Children have become the third most profitable illegal commodity, preceded only by drugs and weapons (Arlacchi 2000). Further, it has been estimated that human sex trafficking, in general, is the fastest expanding business of criminal enterprises and organized crime (Bump and Duncan 2003; Hodge and Lietz 2007; Schauer and Wheaton 2006; Walker-Rodriguez and Hill 2011).

CSEC is frequently understood to be an umbrella term; other crimes "are sometimes placed under the rubric of CSEC" (Mitchell et al. 2011, p. 45). CSEC is a general categorization that includes more specific forms of commercialized sexual abuse such as child trafficking, prostitution, pornography, and sex tourism (Bolling and Harper 2007; Scarpa 2006). In addition to these more commonly researched forms of CSEC, the traveling of child offenders and the subsequent enticement of youth to engage in illegal sexual activity is a form of exploitation underrepresented in research; however, it represents a significant threat to youth. The following sections explore the aforementioned categories of CSEC. However, we first examine characteristics of victims coerced into CSEC to provide the framework for understanding the offender characteristics and mechanisms by which CSEC threatens youth in America.

Chapter 3
Victimology

An exploration of CSEC requires an assessment of victims. In order to understand the crime, it is imperative to identify the risk factors and vulnerabilities associated with victimization. Not surprisingly, child trafficking, prostitution, pornography, and sex tourism share common victim trajectories and characteristics. Overall, young victims of exploitation appear relatively similar across age, gender, and racial groups; however, variations exist between male and female victims. Additionally, different vulnerability factors can be attributed to international victims compared to domestic youth.

Female children are at greater risk for commercial sexual exploitation than male youth (Boxil and Richardson 2007; Estes and Weiner 2001; Fong and Cardoso 2010). Studies have found that the average age in which female youth enter into prostitution is between 12 and 14 years of age (Walker-Rodriguez and Hill 2011). However, girls as young as 9 years of age and boys beginning at 6 years have also been victims of CSEC (Palmer and Stacey 2002). These young ages reflect an overall trend in the commercial sex trade in which there is a demand for increasingly younger victims (Spangenberg 2001). In addition, a variety of races are also victimized by perpetrators of CSEC. For example, some research suggests that Caucasian victims are the primary targets of CSEC; however, other studies have found that African-American and Latino children experience higher rates of victimization (Finklehor and Ormrod 2004; Halter 2010; Spangenberg 2001). While not empirically validated, anecdotal information from law enforcement suggests that the racial breakdown of victims is more specific to the crime. For example, experience suggests that a significant proportion of child prostitution victims are minorities, usually African-American females. In contrast, the vast majority of child pornography images and movies involve Caucasian children. Further, the growing number of international victims brought to the US contributes to the ethnic diversity of CSEC victims. Therefore, it can be assumed that the rate at which different racial groups are victimized is continuously changing and not yet clearly understood.

Domestic Victims

American-born youth are susceptible to a variety of early environmental factors that appear to contribute to their vulnerability. Exploited children frequently experience histories of early exposure to turbulent households. Family problems including neglect, exposure to excessive arguing, violence, or abuse are common experiences of childhood victims of exploitation (Brannigan and Van Bruschot 1997; Fong and Cardoso 2010; Melrose, Barnett, & Bodie 1999; Pearce 2003; Taylor-Browne et al. 2000). There are a variety of hypotheses suggesting why youth from dysfunctional homes are at risk for victimization. First, histories of abuse and neglect may increase a child's likelihood of running away from home (Adelson 2008; Brannigan and Van Brunschot 1997). Research has consistently shown that runaways are targeted by traffickers, pimps, and other offenders (Estes and Weiner 2001; Finklehor and Ormrod 2004). Second, abused and neglected youth may be drawn toward antisocial peers and pressured to engage in delinquent activities such as truancy, experimental drug use, and sexual promiscuity (Chase and Statham 2004). Children who are drawn to antisocial peers in search of acceptance unwittingly expose themselves to potential perpetrators. For example, a minor may engage in prostitution to support a drug habit developed through a delinquent lifestyle (Walker-Rodriguez and Hill 2011).

Despite the proposed theories, research consistently shows that youth trajectories into exploitation most frequently include prior histories of childhood abuse. Victims of childhood sexual exploitation often reveal that their abuse began at home (US Department of Justice, 2007). Pearce (2003) discovered that female youth at risk for forced prostitution were most likely exploited in their earlier lifestyle and relationships. Additionally, Melrose et al. (1999) found that out of their 50 interviews with female prostitutes, the majority of whom entered into prostitution before the age of 18, 72 % of the women endorsed a history of family abuse; and 42 % stated that their first sexual experience was characterized by abuse. As offered by one victim of child prostitution:

> I turned my first date when I was 15 years old. My dad had been molesting me for years, threatening me. I wanted out. Hooking was very liberating. I had control over my life for the first time (Hanna, 2002, p. 16).

The abuse by her father was a priming factor in her future victimization. The repeated sexual abuse catalyzed this child to change her circumstances. Unfortunately, sex was the only currency she had available, thus leaving her vulnerable to the coercion of traffickers and pimps.

As mentioned above, a lack of family support and/or enduring abuse likely precipitates a child's running away from home. From the victim's perspective, running away from home may be the only alternative in searching for safety and acceptance (Adelson 2008). Runaway or homeless youth, who are forced into the child welfare system, are at an increased risk for becoming victims of exploitation (Fong and Cardoso 2010; Walker-Rodriguez and Hill 2011). Exploiters prey on the vulnerability of abandoned and abused youth. They target those with deficient home lives and present the façade of a safe, secure, and loving environment.

Traffickers and pimps assume various roles in an effort to lure their victims. Through a review of case studies and interviews with young victims, it appears that offenders may play the role of an absentee parent or pretend to be a loyal boyfriend. Both personas are used to deceive the victim by providing false promises of unconditional love and acceptance while simultaneously isolating victims from their previous support networks. Vulnerable children and adolescents easily succumb to the manipulation of traffickers and pimps as they are provided sustenance and shelter, blinded by the desire to leave their situation behind for a better life. Behind the carefully crafted facade, these victims find themselves physically and sexually abused and in conditions no better from what they escaped.

Research has also shown a strong relationship between a child's socioeconomic status and vulnerability to exploitation (Chase and Statham 2004; Pearce 2003). Poverty plays an interesting and complex role in the exploitation of youth. While some children are kidnapped, abducted, or sold into the sex trade, impoverished youth may be motivated to voluntarily join the commercial sex industry as a means of sustaining themselves (Melrose et al. 1999). Children and adolescents may resort to a form of "survival sex" in which they exchange sexual favors to provide for their basic needs such as food or shelter (Finklehor and Ormrod 2004; Mitchell et al. 2001; Phoenix 2002). A victim may also use prostitution as a financial means of providing themselves a lifestyle that they could not have obtained otherwise (Taylor-Browne et al. 2002). This could include earning money for materialistic objects or affording a life that an abusive or neglectful home could not provide.

The following example further illustrates the role of early environmental and social factors on a minor's susceptibility to victimization. Dalla (2000) conducted multiple interviews with adult prostitutes in an effort to identify patterns of commonalities for future policy and prevention efforts. The following is an excerpt from one interview.

> Barb was petite, 30 years old and pregnant with her seventh child when she was interviewed. Beginning early in their lives, she and her older sister were molested by their mother and her male friends (Barb believed it started when she was 2). Although other family members were aware of the abuse, no one stepped into protect her. When asked her feelings about it she commented, "I don't need to cry about it the rest of my life; if it happened, then it happened. Apparently it didn't have any impact on my life that I know of." When her parents divorced at age 12 her mother promised Barb and her sisters that she would be back for them, but her mother never returned. Barb ran away at age 13 because she was "in love"; she prostituted for the first time at age 15. In that same year she was also raped by her sister's husband and had her first child...Most of her clients were Sugar Daddies or regulars, and condom use was infrequent...She explained, "When I was emancipated [at 15], as far as family went, I really didn't have one" (p. 7).

Male Victims

Young female victims are disproportionately exploited through the commercialized sex trade. Consequently, the majority of empirical research on child exploitation focuses on the plight of female victims. However, male youth are also involved in

CSEC. Fong and Cardoso (2010) estimate that males comprise roughly 2 % of the commercial sex industry; however, Spangenberg (2001) estimates that boys form a significantly larger minority. These numbers represent the general inconsistencies in reporting the number of male victims.

Male victims typically avoid reporting their victimization, thus contributing to the inaccurate estimates of exploitation. There are a variety of reasons why male victims choose not to reveal their abuse, including the fear of stigmatization. Boys coerced into prostitution frequently have to defend or mask their sexual preferences. Essential to the underreporting of victimized male youth is the fear of the accusation of homosexuality (Spangenberg 2001). An alternative hypothesis is that gay youth may be afraid to be "outed" during the report of their victimization. Additionally, the solicitation of male youth is conducted in such a way that victims are unlikely to be identified. For example, sexual transactions between offenders and male youth tend to occur covertly, taking place in public toilets, bus stops, parks, and public shopping areas or arcades, making it far more difficult to identify victimized males (Chase and Statham 2005; Donovan 1991; Fong and Cardoso 2010).

Identifying trends unique to male victims has implications for physicians, clinicians, law enforcement, and other agencies. Specifically, the process by which male victims of CSEC are identified and provided services needs to be tailored to their unique experiences. For example, boys tend to enter into prostitution at a younger age than females (Palmer 2001). Consequently, males tend to demonstrate a much quicker "aging out" process, leaving the sex trade by their early 20s, whereas female youth may continue to be exploited far into their early adult years (Chase and Statham 2004; Palmer 2001). Further research suggests a correlation between boys' exposure to early exploitation and future involvement in pimping or abusing other vulnerable youth (Chase and Statham 2004). Importantly, there is a gap in the research addressing this subpopulation of victims. Consequently, a more directed focus on this subpopulation has implications and is essential not only for young male victims, but also for future victims of sex crimes and prostitution as well.

International Victims

International victims also play an integral role in the exploitation of children in the US. Not only will these children suffer abuse, but they are also exposed to a variety of hazards characteristic of human trafficking. The US Department of State, *Trafficking in Person's Report* (2004) commented on the various risks inherent to trafficking victims:

> Victims of trafficking often endure brutal conditions that result in physical, sexual, and psychological trauma. Sexually transmitted infections, pelvic inflammatory disease, and HIV/AIDS are often the result of forced prostitution. Anxiety, insomnia, depression, and post-traumatic stress disorder are common psychological manifestations among

trafficked victims. Unsanitary and crowded living conditions, coupled with poor nutrition, foster a host of adverse health conditions such as scabies, tuberculosis, and other communicable diseases. Children suffer growth and development problems and develop complex psychological and neurological consequences from deprivation and trauma (p. 15).

Included in the preceding list is the possibility that victims could die as a direct result of their trafficking. In fact, approximately 400–500 individuals die each year as a consequence of attempting to illegally cross the US–Mexico border alone (Walters and Davis 2011). Moreover, these numbers only represent reported deaths.

Victims of international trafficking generally range from 2 to 17 years of age with the largest concentration of children falling between the ages of 14–17 years (Bump 2009; Fong and Cardoso 2010). An analysis by Bump (2009) pointed to Mexico and Honduras as the largest export countries of trafficked children. China, El Salvador, Guatemala, Southeast Asia, Eastern Europe, and Morocco were also identified as large export contributors (Fong and Cardoso 2010). Originating countries for international victims share some commonalities. For example, they may be underdeveloped and characterized by economic and political upheaval. Deplorable conditions and poverty increase victims' vulnerability to traffickers' manipulation. Origin countries may also be hubs of international transit. As previously mentioned, the globalization of transport markets not only facilitates the trafficking of child victims across international borders, but it also expedites the import of sexual offenders. The international nature of these crimes makes it difficult to prosecute perpetrators and rescue victims. For example, some countries do not recognize the trafficking of children as a crime, thus making it challenging for law enforcement to collaborate and intercept internationally trafficked youth. Further, some countries have legalized prostitution and lowered the age of consent creating an additional barrier to the cessation of international child crimes.

Despite differences in countries of origin or variation in legislation protecting victims, international trafficking victims share similar risk factors with domestically trafficked and coerced children. For example, like their North American counterparts, international victims are likely to come from homes that lack familial support and are characterized by physical or sexual abuse (Robinson 1997). Further, international victims frequently share the same low socioeconomic status as domestic victims. International victims tend to come from impoverished countries and exceptionally poor families. Some youth are thrown out from their family's homes and forced to live on the streets where they become easy targets for traffickers. Other families sell their children, or willingly hand them over to traffickers, who promise the opportunity for a better life (Estes and Weiner 2001).

Minors crossing international borders are also vulnerable to trafficking. Minors traveling into the US unsuspectingly rely on traffickers to arrange for their sponsorship and transportation (Walters and Davis 2011). Regardless if victims have legal documentation or are illegally smuggled across borders, traffickers use the passage to exploit them. Bump (2009) found that both unaccompanied minors and minors accompanied by family members were at risk for trafficking. Minors who were traveling unaccompanied at the time of trafficking were generally older, ranging from 13 to 17 years of age. Youth that were trafficked with family members showed more variation in age, ranging from 2 to 17 years (Bump 2009). Regardless of their age, once minors arrive in the US, they find themselves in debt to their traffickers. With no other means of livelihood, they are forced into prostitution and various other forms of exploitation to pay off their debt. Not surprisingly, the majority of victimized youth remain indebted to their traffickers and pimps well into adulthood.

Once established in the US, trafficked children are often identifiable based on specific features. For example, trafficking victims will demonstrate little knowledge of their surrounding community and will often lack personal possessions, financial records, and a permanent residence. Both domestic and imported victims may show visible signs of torture, malnourishment, beating, or branding. Finally, trafficking victims have extremely limited access to methods of communication and transportation, restricted access to their travel and identification papers and may have a third party that insists on translating for them (Walker-Rodriguez and Hill 2011).

Other factors that increase vulnerability include originating from countries with high crime rates or political corruption, which often facilitate the organized crime rings involved in child trafficking (Schauer and Wheaton 2006). Further, children living near international borders are at risk because of the convenience that it offers traffickers; research suggests that many cities along the Mexican-American border have more relaxed travel restrictions which may facilitate the trafficking of youth (Estes and Weiner 2001). Trafficked children may also lack educational opportunities in their originating countries (Schauer and Wheaton 2006). Lack of education and job skills decreases the likelihood that exploited youth can escape from their abuse once imported into a new country.

Overall, both international and domestic victims share common life trajectories into the CSEC. Exploiters and traffickers target children and youth who are marginalized from society. Often, these children are referred to as "throwaway kids." These victims typically experience difficult home lives, characterized by neglect and abandonment. Likewise, throwaway kids endorse histories of abuse which also increases their likelihood of seeking love, acceptance, or economic resources from potentially dangerous sources. Ultimately, these victims are targeted for their lack of community and family ties.

The following sections will address the various crimes that characterize CSEC. Despite the variability in motive, mechanism, and perpetrators within each crime, similarities across CSEC victims are clearly evident. CSEC is a complicated phenomenon in which crimes overlap, are interconnected, and often dependent on each other to sustain the child sex industry.

Chapter 4
Child Trafficking

The term CSEC is frequently equated with child trafficking. Children who are trafficked may find themselves involved in prostitution, pornography, child labor, domestic servitude, debt bondage, street begging, drug trafficking, service in armed conflicts, illegal adoptions, and organ trafficking (Scarpa 2006). Therefore, it is appropriate to begin discussing the intricacies of CSEC with a careful exploration of what constitutes child trafficking, traffickers, and the mechanism by which it occurs and remains undetected by law enforcement.

According to the United Nations Convention against Transnational Organized Crime and the Protocols (2000), trafficking is defined as

> the recruitment, transportation, transfer, harbouring or receipt of persons, by means of the threat or use of force or other forms of coercion, of abduction, of fraud, of deception, of the abuse of power or of a position of vulnerability or of the giving or receiving of payments or benefits to achieve the consent of a person for the purpose of exploitation (p. 42).

Most broadly, trafficking can be divided into two categories: (1) cross-border international trafficking and (2) internal trafficking within the borders of a country or state (Candappa 2003; Chase and Statham 2004). For our purposes, trafficking is distinguished from smuggling. Where the former implies coercion or manipulation, smuggling more aptly refers to a participant's willingness to move illegally across borders. Due to the debate surrounding a minor's capacity to provide sufficient legal consent, the activities of moving children across borders will be referred to as trafficking.

As domestic trafficking has only recently gained attention, little empirical research has been directed toward quantifying the number of youth trafficked within the US. Additionally, data on international trafficking are ambiguous at best. For example, some researchers suggest that between 14,500 and 17,500 people are trafficked into the US, annually (e.g., US State Departments *Trafficking in Person's Report*). However, as previously asserted, if human trafficking is the third most profitable venture of organized crime, it is likely that the numbers far exceed these conservative estimates (Arlacchi 2000; Bump and Duncan 2003).

Offender Characteristics

Offenders who traffic children for the intent of sexual exploitation come in a variety of forms (Hughes 2008; Walters and Davis 2011; Walker-Rodriguez and Hill 2011). As most of the research surrounding sex trafficking focuses on the victim, data on characteristics of offenders are minimal. However, research has shown a wide range of social and demographic variability among traffickers. These offenders can include individuals or organizations; they can be foreign or domestic born, and they can include members of the racial majority or minority. Traffickers are not always men; women have also been reported to manage international trafficking rings (Sarrica 2009; Walker-Rodriguez and Hill 2011). For example, Sarrica (2009) found that European data reflect an international trend suggesting a higher rate of female perpetrated trafficking than for other crimes, in general. Importantly, however, females still represent a minority of offenders although their numbers are growing. Traffickers can also be "independent contractors, pimps, sexual predators, and diplomats as well as neighbors, friends, and relatives. Some of these criminals are situational, meaning that they engage in trafficking on a limited or one-time basis, while others are full-time purveyors of humans as commodities" (Walters and Davis 2011, p. 6). Very few commonalities exist among traffickers to assist law enforcement in the identification of these offenders. For example, most traffickers have legal status in the US in order to facilitate both domestic and international trade. As many belong to organized crime affiliates or gangs, they frequently traffic guns, weapons, and drugs along with children (Bertone 2000; Walters and Davis 2011; Wyler and Siskin 2010).

The classification of traffickers is further complicated by the variety of roles offenders can assume. The US Department of Justice (2007) identified seven possible roles of child traffickers. These roles include the following: (1) Investors or "arrangers" who provide money for trafficking operations and oversee the criminal enterprise; (2) Recruiters who find the children and may collect fees from their families; (3) Transporters who move the children through the origin, transit, and destination countries; (4) Public officials who receive bribes to provide identity documents and facilitate exiting and entering countries; (5) Informers who gather information on border surveillance, law enforcement activities, and immigration and transit procedures; (6) Debt collectors in destination countries who collect trafficking fees, which can be $30,000 or more per person; (7) Money movers who launder trafficking proceeds (US Department of Justice 2007, p. 6).

There is another, infrequently addressed, dimension to the conceptualization of trafficking organizations: the "bottom." The "bottom" is described as the top of the hierarchy among trafficked and exploited youth. The "bottom" is typically an older adolescent female who acts as the pimp's right hand. She is responsible for disciplining and grooming the girls as well as handling the day-to-day business needs of the trafficker (Petrunov 2011; Walker-Rodriguez and Hill 2011). She does not receive a percentage of funds earned by other girls, but is instead awarded the benefit of receiving a portion of her own earnings. Her position is frequently rewarded with the pimp's affection or through the delegation of more power. A 15-year-old victim describes her daily responsibility as a "bottom":

> He doesn't really go to any of the other girls' hotels, because I collect their money already, so really the only hotel he comes to is mine...I usually collect Cherry's money first, because she usually is right there with me...and then me and her get in the cab and we go over to Tootsie's [where] Barbie and Gigi and Mocha stay...I usually collect their money, I give them some money to get something to eat...[then] I go collect Amber, Tracy, and Strawberry's money...and then I take the rest of the money...I count it and I wait for him to come.

Becoming a "bottom" affords prostitutes agency, power, and control. Although the "bottom" aligns herself with the exploiter and consequently, reaps some benefits, she is still subject to his abuse and violence (Petrunov 2011). Often overlooked, the "bottom" is frequently a victim of trafficking who has used seniority to gain the trust of the offender. Therefore, law enforcement professionals find themselves in the precarious position of negotiating the roles of victim versus offender.

Mechanism of Child Trafficking

The unfortunate reality of child trafficking is that there continues to be a demand for children to exploit (Scarpa 2006). The growing demand for children as a commodity perpetuates a lucrative, underground market. More specifically, the system works because consumers continue to buy sex from children (Scarpa 2006). The disenfranchised nature of trafficking victims enables their perpetual servitude and service to consumers thereby increasing the demand and continuing the cycle of coercion, abuse, and trafficking.

Traffickers target children from all over the world to transport to the US. According to Estes and Weiner (2001), 70 % of foreign-born children trafficked into this country enter on some type of visa, while the other 30 % enter without inspection. A majority of these children come from Mexico and Central America, but many are shipped from Asia, Africa, and the successor states to the former Soviet Union (Bump et al. 2005; Estes and Weiner 2001). Once in the US, traffickers will confiscate all forms of identification such as passports, birth certificates, and drivers licenses. Without legal documents, victims are stranded with no legal identification, ability to return home, or capacity to support themselves (Hughes 2000; Walker-Rodriguez and Hill 2011; Walters and Davis 2011).

Internationally and domestically exploited children are targeted because of their economic status, social standing, or familial relationships. Some children are coerced or abducted while others are controlled through the use of violence, drugs, social isolation, and other forms of exploitation and coercion (Fong and Cardoso 2010; Williams and Frederick 2009). As previously discussed, some parents will pay traffickers to illegally smuggle their children into the US (Aronowitz 2001; Walters and Davis 2011; Vayrynen 2003). While desperate parents attempt to secure a better life for their children, they are unwittingly authorizing passage into sex trafficking and sexual exploitation: "These smugglers/traffickers deceive and dupe the girls through false promises of jobs and other economic opportunities waiting for them in the US… given clothes, makeup, and gifts" (Walters and Davis 2011, p. 3). Upon arrival into the US, these victims are forced into prostitution, domestic servitude, or forced labor. However, this is only one mechanism by which children become trafficked. Offenders reportedly use the Internet, social networking sites, telephone chatlines, and other students to recruit young victims; they may also target youth at malls, schools, and after school activities (Walters and Davis 2011).

Trafficked youth are often coerced into remaining with traffickers and continue in the sex trade through physical and psychological abuse (Williams and Frederick 2009). Offenders also ensure their compliance by separating them from families and friends. The nature of the sex trade and child trafficking does not provide victims with the opportunity to establish positive relationships with others. This isolation, combined with the manipulation by the offender, effectively solidifies the bond between victim and trafficker (Burke 2012; de Fabrique et al. 2007; Walker-Rodriguez and Hill 2011). Burke (2012) defined Stockholm syndrome as "a psychological phenomenon wherein hostages experience and express empathy and positive feelings for their captors… [It] is more likely to develop with children than with adults… [and] reduces the victim's likelihood of acting out, thereby making it easier for the trafficker to exercise control" (p. 17). Further, offenders frequently use sex, drugs, or violent threats to manipulate youth into obedience (Walker-Rodriguez and Hill 2011; Williams and Frederick 2009). Offenders utilize a variety of abusive tactics to keep victims malleable and dependent. Offenders effectively silence their victims by instilling fear and intimidation resulting in the perpetuation of trafficking and sexual exploitation.

Case Example 1: Sex Trafficking Risk Factors

This example highlights the mechanisms of how children and youth become involved in sex trafficking. This victim's story personifies how social and economic factors can create vulnerability for child trafficking. Further, this case illustrates the complexities of trafficking cases. Trafficked victims often suffer concurrent abuse, violence, and future exploitation. This victim's story poignantly underscores how CSEC crimes overlap as she found herself both trafficked and unwillingly inducted into child prostitution.[1]

Amber was 13 years old when she was identified during an investigation as a possible victim of child trafficking and prostitution. Amber had a difficult upbringing: she was born to a 14-year-old mother, lived below the poverty line, and had a

---

[1] Importantly, the names of the victims and offenders have been changed for purposes of this review in order to protect the victims from identification and re-victimization.

history of truancy, delinquency, and risky sexual behaviors. During an interview with FBI agents, Amber reported that:

> She did not have a good relationship with her mother and explained that her mother had told her that if she was going to have sex, she might as well 'get paid' for it.

As a consequence of her callous upbringing, Amber turned to a life of prostitution.

> At 13 years of age, Amber worked in a nightclub called 'Angels'... [The club's manager] knew that Amber was a minor but allowed her to dance, strip, and 'trick' at the club. [He also] engaged in sexual intercourse with Amber in exchange for allowing her to work there without any paperwork.

By 15 years of age, Amber had been arrested over 15 times. Her charges included trespassing, vandalism, loitering, prostitution, resisting arrest, battery, probation violations, and aggravated stalking. She had been detained, forced into residential care, and even found herself homeless. She abused alcohol, marijuana, and cocaine and had a history of psychiatric hospitalizations. Amber's history of delinquency, involvement in the foster care system, troubled home life, substance abuse, and psychiatric difficulties placed her at exponential risk of becoming exploited. Amber was a "throwaway kid."

In October, 2004, Amber ran away from home. She was solicited by pimp partners Double D and Slick. Double D and Slick convinced Amber to enter the "lifestyle."

> [Double D] taught her the rules of the "Game" and how much to charge for various sex acts ($50 for a blow job and $100 for sexual intercourse). Amber stated that she did not make very much money while working for Double D, as she was new to the Game.

After one week working the "track" for Double D, Amber began having problems with his "bottom." Double D sold Amber to his pimp partner, Slick, and placed her on a Greyhound bus from Florida to Tennessee. Slick then transferred Amber from Tennessee to Arkansas where she worked as a prostitute at multiple truck stops.

> While working, Amber wore women's clothing that Slick provided for her...On a daily basis, they used marijuana that Slick provided. She could not remember if Big Daddy [another pimp that Amber worked for] engaged in sexual intercourse with her, but did remember that she performed oral sex on him.

For 18 months, Amber was sold to approximately 17 pimps and trafficked across the US Amber reported that she endured beatings and sexual assault from her new "daddies" and their "bottom" girls. Her pimps used violence, sexual abuse, coercion, and drugs to keep her locked into a lifestyle of prostitution.

Approximately two years later, Amber was recovered by law enforcement. She initially refused to give a statement as she had developed a perverse sense of loyalty toward her pimps. Even though they beat, abused, and sexually assaulted her, the pimps provided shelter, food, and a sense of family. She eventually cooperated with investigators and helped law enforcement bring down a network of pimps across the county.

Slick was charged and subsequently sentenced to a prison term of 6 years and 6 months for transporting a minor across state lines with the intent to engage in illegal sexual activity and with inducing a minor to engage in illicit sex. Double D was charged and subsequently sentenced to a prison term of 5 years and 3 months for transporting a minor across state lines with the intent to engage in illegal sexual activity.

Chapter 5
Child Prostitution

Child prostitution is the commodification and coercion of a child to perform sexual acts. Typically, these acts are exchanged for money; however, sexual acts may also be exchanged for other forms of payment or barter. Child prostitution falls under the legal dimension of CSEC, because it includes the coercion of a child who is economically, cognitively, psychologically, and socially vulnerable to offenders and consumers (Chase and Statham 2004; Lim 1998). Therefore, child prostitution is considered an egregious violation of human rights and arguably the most deplorable and horrific abuse a child can endure.

Internationally, over one million children are forced into prostitution each year with the total number of victims reaching nearly 10 million. It is estimated that child prostitution is a $20 billion a year industry (Willis and Levy 2002). Domestically, child prostitution is a growing concern as American children are continuing to enter the commercial sex trade. The increasing number of foreign youth being trafficked into the US for the purposes of sexual exploitation warrants additional concern. Unfortunately, children and adolescents involved in prostitution are frequently criminalized; they are branded as delinquents. They are arrested, incarcerated, and charged with prostitution with the unfortunate consequence of society labeling them a sexual deviant and a criminal.

However, the work of nonprofit organizations, such as the National Center for Missing and Exploited Children and the National Council on Crime and Delinquency, have endorsed legislation, policies, and practices which recognize youth in prostitution as victims while offering options for appropriate care. Conceptualizing youth in prostitution as children with few choices who sell sex as a means of survival, more effectively underscores the plight of children coerced into prostitution (US Department of Justice, 2007). Legally, children and adolescents are deemed emotionally, physically, and cognitively immature and, therefore, are unable to consent to sexual acts; however, children and adolescents are continuously victimized by perpetrators and the legal system. Fortunately, a growing number of legal mandates are being enforced to protect minors victimized by the sex industry.

What is frequently missing from the research, however, is law enforcement's perspective on the criminalization of these youth. Law enforcement recognizes the gravity of the youth's experience and acknowledges them as a victim of exploitation, but is often left with few options to maintain the safety and security of the minor. What is often overlooked by researchers and advocates is the grip and authority pimps hold over their victims which creates a climate where they cannot escape even when offered help. Experience has proven that when exploited youth are placed in foster care, group homes, or homeless shelters, they run away and return to the "safety" of their pimps. Therefore, law enforcement may be left with no other option than to detain or charge victims of child prostitution as delinquents in an attempt to protect the minor and secure their testimony for trial. As a result, law enforcement is left with two alternatives to ensure pimps are charged, prosecuted, and convicted: institutionalization or detainment of victims.

Offender Characteristics

There are two main categories of offenders within child prostitution: pimps and johns. The term "pimp" refers to the individual that procures, grooms, and markets a minor for prostitution. "johns" are sexual offenders who solicit sex from minors. Unfortunately, data regarding the specific differences between the two groups are vague. Perhaps more frustratingly, there is little differentiation between individuals who solicit adult prostitutes and those who target youth. In fact, little is known about the "johns" or pimps involved in child prostitution (Hughes et al. 2004). Chase and Statham (2004) suggest the gap in data may be a result of vague conviction categorization. True to this theory, there is no single category that distinguishes the solicitation of prostituted youth from the solicitation of an adult prostitute.

Considering the overlap in CSEC crimes, however, it may be possible to infer characteristics of offenders involved in prostitution are similar to that of other exploiters. "johns" may be similar to other sexual offenders and consumers of child sexual exploitation. They qualify as either situational or preferential abusers. The terms situational and preferential offenders are "label[s] used to identify, for investigative and prosecutive purposes, a certain type of offender" (p. 75). Situational offenders "tend to be less intelligent and overrepresented in lower socioeconomic groups" whose "criminal sexual behavior tends to be in the services of basic sexual needs or nonsexual needs such as power and anger" (Lanning 2008, p. 76). In contrast, the preferential offenders "tend to be more intelligent and are overrepresented in high socioeconomic groups" whose "criminal sexual behavior tends to be in the services of deviant sexual needs" and a preference for a specific type of victim (Lanning 2008, p. 75).

They are most likely males, between late 20s and late 60s, ranging in occupation from blue-collar workers to professionals. Consumers of child prostitution may consider it less risky than other forms of exploitation and may feel a sense of security exploiting forgotten youth; consequently, they may be overtly brutal and look for children to torture or batter (Hughes et al. 2004). McKegany and Bloor (1990) identified consumers of young, male victims as men who were primarily heterosexual married, bisexual, or not openly homosexual. In addition, "johns" and pimps are frequently involved in other serious crimes such a possession and/or sale of drugs and firearms (Duffin 2004).

It may also be helpful for law enforcement to identify offenders by their mechanisms of exploitation and the characteristics of their victims. For example, a pimp may be overtly controlling or aggressive and referred to as a "gorilla pimp." According to law enforcement, these men typically use violence, frequent beatings, and threats of physical harm as the mechanism of control over their victims. On the streets, this tactic is often referred to as "breaking a girl."

Alternatively, the "finesse" pimp assumes the role of the boyfriend using intimacy or sex as a way to solidify power. The girls who work for "finesse" pimps frequently refer to themselves as "wife-in-laws." Finally, the "daddy" pimp uses his ability to provide comfort, sustenance, and protection as a means to coerce children into prostitution. The role becomes so commanding that young victims frequently refer to the pimp and his "bottom" as the "folks." Regardless of the type of pimp, these offenders may be surrounded by young, marginalized females or males that are seemingly dependent on or subservient to them.

Spidel et al. (2006) conducted an archival analysis of Canadian inmates convicted, charged, and/or admitted to at least one "pimping" offense. Their results indicated that pimps ranged in age from 19 to 45 years, and the majorities were Caucasian males. They found that the mean level of education was 9.3 years and that most offenders endorsed a history of prior psychiatric diagnosis and substance abuse. Results also revealed that nearly the entire sample had prior convictions of violent offenses and demonstrated high correlations with psychopathic behaviors and characteristics. Finally, both demographic descriptors found in Spidel et al. (2006) and the experience of American law enforcement suggests that pimps vary in their racial and ethnic backgrounds.

Mechanism of Forced Prostitution

As previously mentioned, children and adolescents can voluntarily join or be trafficked into prostitution. Trafficked victims can be abducted, coerced, pressured, sold by parents to perpetrators, or sold among pimps. They can become entwined in a transnational crime network in which they are repeatedly shipped across state lines for the purpose of sexual exploitation. The mechanism of trafficking is only one of many trajectories by which youth are exploited through prostitution. This section will address the various methods in which offenders coerce children into prostitution.

Offenders groom their victims in a variety of ways. For example, a perpetrator targets a child or teenager lacking familial ties or social support. The offender might demand she/he calls him "daddy," thus solidifying his pseudo-paternal control and decreasing the likelihood that the victim will challenge his authority (Walker-Rodriguez and Hill 2011). Offenders will use romantic relationships and promises of a future to manipulate their victim. For example, the offender offers his young female victim promises of security and love. He refers to himself as her "boyfriend." In an effort to please him, the victim excuses his unwanted sexual advances and succumbs to his pressure to engage in sexual acts with other men (Petrunov 2011; Walker-Rodriguez and Hill 2011).

Other victims find themselves brutally initiated into the sex industry. Violence, beatings, sexual abuse, and gang rape are tools utilized by offenders to intimidate, control, and prevent victims from leaving prostitution (Walker-Rodriguez and Hill 2011; Williams and Frederick 2009). Colloquially, victims that resist their pimp must be "broken." A 14-year-old victim described how her pimp recruited a new, underage female, and subsequently "broke" her into submission after several attempts to escape from a life of child prostitution:

> After a while, [she] just stopped fighting. She tried to run away but he got her again… she tried to run away again, then he got her again, and so she just stopped trying to run away…[when she ran away] he beat her up…he punched her in the eye and then he [made] her sit in a bathtub full of cold water…she couldn't move until she said she wasn't gonna leave anymore…[she] would have been 15.

Similar to trafficking victims, child and adolescent victims of prostitution can develop Stockholm syndrome. Children and adolescents pressured into prostitution form an attachment to the offender despite the history of abuse and violence (Burke 2012; Kendall and Funk 2012; Walker-Rodriguez and Hill 2011). Consequently, prostituted children may develop a perverse bond with their captor that is difficult to fracture, effectively reinforcing the hold perpetrators have over victims. Despite the physical and sexual abuse that 14-year-old "Nancy" suffered at the hands of her pimp, she continued to maintain a morbid love for her abuser:

> Kurby heard [Nancy] crying and screaming. When Kurby entered the room, [Nancy] was laying on the bed and Mark was straddling her, throwing punches to her body. Kurby ran into the room, grabbed [Mark], and threw him off of [Nancy]. [Nancy] was screaming, 'I love you, Mark. I love you, Mark' and was extremely upset with the situation. [Nancy] agreed at that point to go with [Mark].

The offenders frequently provide respite for throwaway youths who are homeless, hungry, and forgotten, effectively leaving them with no other option other than to remain with their abuser.

The commodification of victims' bodies permits offenders to objectify children. This distortion is used to justify continued exploitation and abuse of their victims. It is likely the victim aligns himself/herself with this view and is discouraged from any attempt to escape.

Children in the sex trade lack education, skills, and the support necessary to find work and opportunities outside of prostitution. Lack of resources encourages them back into prostitution or ushers them into other channels of criminal activity (Mikhail 2002). Consequently, the opinion impressed upon society is that "these girls are seen as public goods… [subsequently] they become subjected to physical violence and sexual abuse in the very institutions that are supposed to protect them and help them in the recovery process" (Mikhail 2002, p. 5).

Case Example 2: Methods of Victimization by Child Prostitution

The following example explores one mechanism of how youth find themselves involved child prostitution. The case study of Kasha provides a critical examination of how risk factors, such as disability and lack of educational attainment, can facilitate victimization. Further, her case emphasizes how prior exposure to abuse, specifically a history of sexual abuse, can prime victims for involvement in prostitution. Kasha's perspective identifies methods by which her pimps manipulated and coerced numerous child victims into prostitution. Her story also exemplifies how victims of child prostitution become both commodities and tools to secure more victims and perpetuate the child sex trade.

At 16 years of age, Kasha was arrested for juvenile prostitution. She was a legally blind, African-American girl, with a 5th grade education. In her statement to authorities, she described her troubled past which facilitated her entry into prostitution:

> When I was four, my dad started touching me ...that went on to about seven-eight, when I told my mom, she didn't believe me...I told her the complete truth about what happened, and she didn't believe me, so it kind of caused problems between me and her from the age of nine to maybe 13, and...I met a man [B-Kul] and...he told me that he managed girls and he ...helped girls get theirselves together and if I wanted to be a part of it, I could come...

Five years prior, Kasha met B-Kul online. They maintained communications via Internet and telephone through which B-Kul invited her to travel to his hometown. B-Kul began grooming Kasha by appealing to her emotions through continued conversations and sending her money. She likely viewed B-Kul as an escape from violence and abuse subsequently increasing her trust in him. With the money he sent via wire transfer, Kasha purchased a round-trip bus ticket to see him. She stated that she stayed one day and did not have sexual intercourse with B-Kul, at this time. At this point in their relationship, Kasha likely felt protected and safe rather than exploited.

Kasha and B-Kul continued to maintain contact with each other and three months later, B-Kul drove to a neighboring state to see her. In her statement to law enforcement, Kasha recalled the grooming process in more detail:

> ...he told me that he was a pimp, and he started explaining like what his lifestyle was about, what his girls do, and uhm, he asked me did I want to come with him. And at the time, I really didn't understand what he was talking about ...but I liked him so I went with him.

B-Kul purchased a bus ticket for Kasha, while he drove with his pimp partner to New York. B-Kul instructed Kasha to leave all of her stuff behind and that he would "get [her] all new stuff," thereby contributing to her complete reliance on him. B-Kul effectively isolated Kasha from her home, family, and entire life. She described the beginning of her relationship with B-Kul:

> We were hanging out, we were having sex, he was buying me stuff...most of the time he was trying to instruct me like, well you got to do it this way, or you have to do it that way...And then, four days into it, he told me I either had to go to work or I had to leave, leave everything that he gave me and go back to Willingboro, and...I had to find my own way back...he wasn't gonna pay for my ticket.

Kasha "tricked" for B-Kul out of various motels and was instructed on how to "work the track" by B-Kul's "bottom" girl, Luscious. Kasha eventually became jealous of the attention B-Kul paid to Luscious so, Kasha "chased her off."

B-Kul then trafficked Kasha from the east coast to the west coast of the US. While in the west coast, B-Kul used drugs to coerce another minor female victim into prostitution:

> It's a drink called Lean...he gave some to [minor female victim] and he kind of kidnapped her from the strip club...it knocks you out completely...you don't wake up for a couple of hours after drinking Lean...he uses it to get girls...if he pimps out a girl and the girl doesn't you know, show him any effort or any, any type of attention, ...he'll put a little bit of Lean in their Sprite...he'll make them become his ho, basically...

For four years, B-Kul recruited two additional minor female victims, ages 11 (Cherry) and 15 (Unidentified). B-Kul had a total of four minor females "working" for him.

Kasha illustrated how B-Kul would beat them when they did something wrong. For example, she stated,

> I wear glasses...B-Kul broke 'em...because he got mad because another pimp told him that I was reckless eyeballing at him. So he said if you can't see then you won't be able to reckless eyeball... [And] one time he kicked me in my eye...and he didn't let me work at all for maybe two weeks, because my eye was swollen.

She also witnessed B-Kul physically assault the other minor female victims. In her statement to law enforcement, she stated that B-Kul used an iron to beat Cherry and pushed her down a flight of stairs, resulting in a broken arm.

B-Kul also used other forms of degradation against the victims. Kasha described how B-Kul would "share" her with his pimp partners and brand her with his pimp names:

> He forced me to get [the tattoos]...He took me to the tattoo parlor, and he made me sit there, and he told me If I ...screamed or I flinched or anything, when we got home he was gonna beat me

At 14, Kasha gave birth to her first child, who was fathered by B-Kul. She reported that B-Kul would use her son as a means of controlling her. She also expressed concerns that her son would continue the cycle of victimization that she was trapped in:

> Because he always comes and finds me and he always comes and, and takes me away and...or he'll hold my son against me. My son is with him now...he doesn't let me...I'm only allowed to see my son on Sundays. That's my day off...he'll take him on the track and let him walk around, and talk to all the other pimps like he's grown and, it's just

horrible, and he won't let me see my son, and I can't even take care of my son, and he's obviously not doing a good job taking care of my son, so I would like for my son to get taken away from him before he grows up to be a pimp...

For four years, Kasha was trafficked in nine states. She was put to work on railroad tracks, in casinos, and on Craig's list. She reported that B-Kul solicited another pimp to create false identification for him, her, and the other minor female victims to facilitate their travel.

Cherry was also eventually arrested for juvenile prostitution. She identified B-Kul as her pimp and reported his location to authorities which resulted in a raid of the motel where they were staying. Two of the minor female victims lied about their age; however, Kasha told authorities her actual age and was taken into custody. Cherry and Kasha were placed in a group home. Charges against B-Kul were dropped due to insufficient evidence, and B-Kul arrived at the group home to pick both girls up. Kasha reported that they were beaten for telling on him.

Later, Cherry and Kasha were arrested for a second time. Authorities were aware of their Division of Youth and Family Services case, and they were sent back to the state in which the case had been originally opened. Kasha reported that her case was eventually dismissed. She described her frustration and disappointment with the legal system and why she continued to return to her pimp:

> ...I tried to stay in the group home, you know, but the man at the group home started touching me, so they moved me to another group home, but the girls there were all crazy and wild and wanted to fight all the time, so they moved me back to my first original group home, and I was like well hey...nobody's doing nothing for me, he came once again, sweet talking me, so I went back to him again.

As part of her statement, Kasha's closing words were a painful demonstration of the never-ending cycle that continues to trap child victims into the world of prostitution. She listed her goals for the future that were virtually unattainable while her abuser continued to be free. Likewise, despite the abuse that she endured, she also described the love that she had for her abuser:

> Well, first I have to get away from him; if I don't see him then I won't have the urge to go back to him. So...once I get away from him, then I can work on getting my G.E.D. and going to college and getting a trade and getting a job and maybe one day I can get my son back. But until that day when somebody actually gets B-Kul...off the streets, he's always gonna keep having girls through this whole process, getting locked up, he does bond them out or they get released to juvenile e home and we go right back to him... if nobody else is helping us, why should we help ourselves....I do love him. Yes, I do love him...For the, the strange world of ... pimping and hoeing, yes he treats me well, but for a normal society life, no. Because someone who you love the way I love him, wouldn't be making me do something like this.

Two years later, Kasha cooperated with law enforcement and spent approximately 20 hours providing a statement, identifying other victims, and assisting with efforts to locate B-Kul. However, similar to many other victims, Kasha was socially disadvantaged and scarred by a history of abuse. Kasha ultimately returned to a life of child prostitution.

Importantly, this case example parallels the anecdotal experience of law enforcement. Often, victims, who are placed in group homes and foster care, escape and return to their pimps or their pimps physically retrieve them from these "safe havens." Law enforcement actively voices their frustration that the perverse bond and loyalty that these victims experience puts them back into dangerous situations and prevents them from testifying in court resulting in the continued victimization of children.

Chapter 6
Pornography

Pornography differs from other forms of sexual exploitation in which the victim does not always come into direct contact with consumers. Rather, victims are made to perform lewd and lascivious acts, such as genital exhibition, masturbation, oral, anal, genital sex, sadomasochism, or bestiality, while the offender documents their sexual activity. Child pornography is any material which depicts real or simulated explicit sexual activities that involve a child (Chase and Statham 2004; Finklehor 1994; Graham 2000). This form of exploitation creates an international underground and highly profitable industry. Child pornography has proven to be a rapidly growing $20 billion industry, threatening the safety of at-risk American children (Bourke and Hernandez 2009). The availability and affordability of computers, recent technological advancements, accessibility of the Internet, and the development of Webcams have contributed to the overall growth and success of the child pornography industry. According to the 2006 Congressional testimony of Michelle Collins, Director of Exploited Child Unit for the National Center for Missing and Exploited Children, "the number of reports of online enticement of children… increased 400 % since 1998." Similarly, between 1996 and 2006, the FBI's Innocent Images National Initiative reported a 2,026 % increase in cases of child pornography (FBI 2006). The following sections will explore the unique mechanism of child pornography including the creation, distribution, and consumption of sexually exploitative images and videos.

Offender Characteristics

The globalization of child pornography and anonymity provided by the Internet makes it difficult for law enforcement and researchers to identify offender characteristics. Research suggests that less is known about child pornography consumers or pornographers than any other type of sexual offender (Bourke and Hernandez 2009; Webb et al. 2007). However, data currently available can assist law enforcement in identifying and targeting populations and individuals that may be involved in child pornography.

Individuals that produce child pornography might do so because they interact with exploited children via trafficking, prostitution, or other mechanisms of abuse. Other producers may be part of organized crime networks or online sharing networks. Still, others might video record or photograph victimized youth under their control in order to trade and distribute "fresh" material among other pornographers. As a result, the characteristics of child pornographers can be difficult to conceptualize. They can be members of sex trafficking rings, gang leaders, family members, neighbors, community leaders, religious figures, or little league coaches. Law enforcement officials, policy makers, and legislators can look to the characteristics of other CSEC offenders and child abusers for a broader picture of child pornographer characteristics. While little is known exclusively about producers of child pornography, more information is available about the consumer of child pornography. While reviewing the following section regarding the child pornography consumer, it is important to remember that the production and consumption of child pornography do not necessarily occur in mutual exclusion. Similar to producers, consumers often collect, produce, and distribute child pornography among other perpetrators.

Consumers are more likely to be employed, in a relationship, better educated, and have a higher IQ than offenders who commit other sexual crimes (Blundell et al., 2002; Schwartz and Southern 2000; and Webb et al. 2007). Child pornographers and consumers can include teachers, professors, celebrities, judges, dentists, and police officers (Calder 2004). They can also be coaches, neighbors, religious leaders, or parents. Other salient characteristics of consumers are that they tend to be white males, in their 30's, and heavy Internet users (Blundell et al. 2002; Schneider 2000; and Webb et al. 2007). Additionally, Webb et al. (2007) found consumers of child pornography were more likely to have endorsed a history of mental health services and have lower rates of substance abuse than other sexual offenders.

A significant amount of empirical data suggests that there is a link between Internet consumption of child pornography and hands-on abuse of children (Bourke and Hernandez 2009; Wolak et al. 2005). In fact, in a recent treatment evaluation of offenders, Bourke and Hernandez (2009) found that 85 % of their sample admitted to child abuse with only 2 % of the sample passing a polygraph confirming involvement in "just pictures." Consequently, some researchers are advocating for the dissolution of monikers, such as "child pornographers," "child abusers," and "pedophiles" because of the similarities, crossover, and overlap between crime and offender (Bourke and Hernandez 2009; Hernandez 2000; Seto et al. 2006; and Wolak et al. 2005). Whether the use of current sex offender labels becomes antiquated, the fact remains that those involved in prior sexual offenses are more likely to view child pornography at higher rates than those who have not (Bourke and Hernandez 2009; Hanson and Bussiere 1998).

Research suggests that these offenders have distinct maladaptive cognitive patterns which allow the perpetrators to justify the crime. More specifically, offenders tend to distort their reality, use fantasy play, and other thinking errors to facilitate and encourage future offending while avoiding responsibility for their actions

(Bourke and Hernandez 2009; Taylor and Quayle 2003). Take for example, an offender that fails to recognize the abuse that the children depicted in his collection of images have endured and subsequently justifies his participation in the victimization process as mere fantasy:

> I am more or less into this for fantasy only. I was in a relationship that did not last and no kids were involved. After that I was lonely and used the Internet for companionship. The screen name I created was to be able to chat with other parents. Again all in fantasy. I have never met anyone of the people I have chatted with. Truthfully, I would not partake in the actions if it ever became available to me....I was alone and just fantasized.

Another common offender distortion is that offenders inadvertently or unintentionally become involved in child pornography (Bourke and Hernandez 2009; Seto Reeves et al. 2010). For example, an offender might claim that the pornographic material was from a pop-up window online, sent by a third party, accessed by accident, or that they were unaware of the child's age. Other offenders claim their consumption of pornographic material is related to a psychological problem like a mood, anxiety, or substance abuse disorder; still, others assert that perusing child pornography helps them "work through their own childhood victimization, or [is an act] of online investigative vigilantism" (Bourke and Hernandez 2009).

While the above information relates to child pornography consumers in general, Krone (2004) further differentiated various types of consumers based on their motivations and modus operandi. Table 6.1 provides an abbreviated typology, adapted from Krone (2004) that identifies these different types of consumers.

Law enforcement schema simplifies the preceding typologies by dividing child pornography offenders into five categories: (1) possessor, (2) distributor, (3) collector, (4) trader, or (5) producer. Additionally, law enforcement refers to the "physical abuser" pornographer as a hands-on offender.

Mechanism of Pornography

In recent years, the mechanism of pornography has evolved with the advancement and popularity of the Internet, chat rooms, and Webcams. The Internet may be better understood as an accelerator for the child pornography industry (Bourke and Hernandez 2009; Chase and Statham 2004; Graham 2000; and Webb et al. 2007). Researchers cite peer-to-peer networks and E-serves as mechanisms which facilitate the fast, private, and mostly undetected transmission of large quantities of pornographic material to offenders on an international level (Burke et al. 2002, Forde and Patterson 1998; Mostyn 2000; and Thornburg and Lin 2002). These platforms allow "predatory offenders to electronically creep into the bedrooms of our nation's youth, where they engage in sexually explicit "chat," "cybervoyeurism" (using the child's Webcam to view him or her in a state of undress or engaged in sexual activity), and 'cyberexhibitionism' (displaying their genitals, via

Table 6.1 Types of child pornography consumers

Browser	A browser is characterized by the unintentional access of child pornography either via span or through accidental use of a suspect site. The browser's level of networking is extremely low as they do not actively seek out child pornography but, in the event that they gain access to it, may decide to keep it. In order to prosecute browsers, authorities must prove intention to possess illicit images of children
Private fantasy	The mere fantasy of engaging in sexual acts with a child does not constitute a prosecutable offense. However, if an individual uses the computer to document their fantasy in written or digital format, a violation has been committed. The Private Fantasy consumer creates child pornography for their own private use. Because this offender has no intention of sharing his material, the use of predatory networking is very low. These consumers are often exposed by third-party individual (e.g., computer repair individuals or suspicious neighbors)
Trawler	Trawlers often use openly available Web browser and employ little or no security when searching for child pornography. The trawler peruses the Internet for child pornography for one of three reasons: (1) they have a variety of sexual interests/fetishes including children, (2) they are sexually curious about children, or (3) they assert their right to access whatever material they deem appropriate. These offenders minimally network with other offenders
Non-secure collector	Non-secure collector employ little security measures to actively seek out child pornography. They use offender networks including predicated chat rooms and peer-to-peer sharing programs, to trade, download, or purchase child pornography
Secure collector	The secure collector compulsively collects child pornography through secure, predicated networks. They take extensive security measures including passwords, encryption codes, and group entry requirements (i.e., each member is required to submit child pornography images to join, thus locking protecting each member from exposure)
Groomer	The groomer uses the Internet to facilitate establishing a sexual relationship with a child. The sexual relationship may be physical or virtual. Additionally, child pornography is used to desensitize the child and promote further exploitation
Physical abuser	The physical abuser is a hands-on offender. This offender is actively involved in the physical abuse of a child. They may digitally document their sexual exploitation of their victims for their personal use. The physical abuser also qualifies as a consumer because they may use child pornography to groom their victims or supplement their sexual urges
Producer	The producer of child pornography is involved in the physical abuse of children. This form of offender is actively involved in the physical abuse of a child. They document the physical torture and sexual exploitation of their victims. These images or videos are then provided to other consumers through predicated networks. The producer may also entice children and adolescents to send him sexually explicit photos of themselves
Distributor	A distributer is directly involved in the sale, trade, sharing, downloading, and exchange of child pornography. They may be preferential offenders that share/provide child pornography with other offenders, or they may be opportunistic abusers that capitalize on the sale of child pornography

the Internet, to a minor)" (Bourke and Hernandez 2009, p. 183). Unfortunately, as technology has evolved, so too has the manner in which offenders seduce, manipulate, and abuse children.

Advancements in the Internet and technology have enabled increased anonymity and faster, more efficient, dissemination of child pornographic material. Additionally, developments in modern software allow for the erasure of electronic footprints and the storage of data in covert corners of the Internet. This new hardware prevents the storage of illicit activities on a computer's hard drive, further protecting the offender from detection (Bourke and Hernandez 2009; Burke et al. 2002; Forde and Patterson 1998; Mostyn 2000; and Thornburg and Lin 2002). Evidence eliminators, such as "shredders," create further avenues for offenders to conceal their crime.

The victim does not typically interface with the consumer in the same manner as a commercially trafficked or prostituted child; however, the traumatic consequences of their exploitation must not be underemphasized. The content produced is inevitably horrific although the manner in which children are coerced into pornography varies. In some instances, producers travel to impoverished countries to purchase children for use in their pornographic material; these children are often manipulated through the use of drugs and are hidden from law enforcement as the producers relocate to various locations (US Department of Justice 2007). Alternatively, producers may target indigent families and convince parents that they can provide their children with education and employment abroad. In an attempt to provide their child the opportunity at a better life or for substantial monetary gain, parents unknowingly hand their children over to pornographers (Healy 1996; U.S. Department of Justice 2007).

Another manner of coercion comes from the intrafamilial producer. Children who are victims of domestic sexual abuse may also be photographed by their abuser (Healy 1996). In fact, Healy (1996) found that nearly 75 % of children depicted in pornography were living in their family home when they were sexually exploited. The unavoidable conclusion is that a large number of sexually exploited and coerced children become victims in their own homes (Estes 2001; U.S. Department of Justice 2007).

Children exploited through pornography encounter multiple traumas. The act of manipulation and coercion has the potential to create negative outcomes, including the following: forced enslavement and isolation, development of drug dependency, or experience of traumatic physical abuse. The child victim suffers sexual abuse resulting from the real or simulated sexual act which is recorded and used for the production of pornographic material (Esposito 1998 and Graham 2000). Further, the offender may use explicit images of the victims as blackmail in order to facilitate their continued exploitation. Finally, pornographic material may also be used to justify ongoing sexual abuse (Graham 2000; Healy 1996; US Department of Justice 2007; and Wasserman 1998). For example, research has shown that both pornographers and consumers use child pornography to seduce and coerce new victims. According to Wasserman (1998), exposure to child pornography "desensitizes the child and lowers his inhibitions… [demonstrating that it is] permissible to engage in sexual conduct… and induce participation by children in sexual conduct" (p. 268).

The pornography industry has proven to be both commercialized and lucrative. Undeniably, pornographers and the supporting criminal networks turn a profit with the sale of child pornographic materials; however, it is also common for consumers to trade images. These traders will exchange rather than pay for pornographic material (Estes 2001; Gillen 2003). In effect, the bartering of images and videos contributes to the continued demand for explicit child images by increasing the circulation of child pornography while simultaneously supporting the framework of the commercial pornography industry (Chase and Statham 2004). From the perspective of researchers and law enforcement, the circulation of child pornography among offenders obscures current definitions. No longer are pornographer and consumer two distinct entities. Now, producers, traders, possessors, collectors, and distributors are nearly indistinguishable in which consumers have also become distributors (Graham 2000). Consequently, "the consumer-trader may be thought of as the mortar that holds the bricks, i.e., the content-producing child pornography operations, together" (Graham 2000, p. 461).

Case Example 3: Consumer, Trader, and Distributor of Child Pornography

A 46-year-old Caucasian male, with a prior arrest record for possession of marijuana and methamphetamines signed on to an Internet chat room under a screen name that highlighted his deviant, sexual preference: He preferred very young children in subservient positions. At the time of his arrest in a child pornography investigation, he was on probation and had mandatory drug screenings. The offender was open about his sexual preference and indicated that he endured a psychologically abusive childhood in which his mother exposed him to sex on a regular basis. Additionally, he reported a history of a severe medical condition which caused him to feel "uncomfortable with sex" and consequently had abstained from sexual intercourse since his diagnosis, 20 years prior.

He indicated that sexual frustration, a need for companionship, and curiosity drew him to child pornography. He admitted to collecting child pornography for approximately 10 years and had accumulated thousands of images and videos. The images and videos contained victims, ranging in age from infants to preteens, often including torture, rape, and other forms of degradation. When asked, "What does child pornography mean to you," he responded,

> The way that I've tried to analyze it or I guess live with it is…it's not something I would act on or do anything. It's, it's up here (points to head), it's like how some people I guess are into animals or how some people are into whatever fetish that they're into. For me, what I've analyzed is…it's about the dominance of the male. I'm not interested in women

with kids. I'm not interest[ed] with kids...it's a dominate male with a younger kid... In my fantasy...it's the man dominating the child.

Law enforcement officers in New Mexico, New York, Missouri, and Florida had previously initiated investigations regarding this offender's online activities. In follow-up to the leads, FBI and police officers conducted an interview and forensic preview of his computer. During this time, he did not make any admissions, and the forensic preview of his computer did not reveal any images or videos containing child pornography. In a subsequent part of the investigation, it was discovered that the offender used various measures to avoid detection by authorities. He had carefully saved images and videos on two thumb drives which remained hidden in a locked safe. He operated under multiple Internet screen names and accessed wireless networks from his neighbors in order to view, trade, and download pornography.

A ruse was orchestrated to catch the offender online during the execution of a search warrant. The ruse was successful, and law enforcement observed his laptop to be on and signed in to the program that he had used to trade child pornography. In addition, one of the offender's thumb drives was connected to the laptop. During his confession, he responded,

> I don't think that people understand that it can be a fantasy without it being a monster. I don't feel like a monster, because I don't go to playgrounds...I don't have anything to do with children. I don't even know people that have children.

Pursuant to a plea agreement, the offender plead guilty to one count of distribution of child pornography and was subsequently sentenced to a prison term of 16 years and 6 months.

This case example demonstrates how child pornographers and collectors minimize their crimes to appear acceptable and normal. For example, this offender, as well as many others, assumes the attitude that viewing images of young children being tortured, raped, and abused is permissible as long as they are not the perpetrators of the actual physical victimization. Additionally, although this offender never admitted to hands-on offending, as previously acknowledged, child pornography can act as a gateway to the sexual assault of accessible victims; hence, the possibility that he may have deceived authorities should not be ignored.

Case Example 4: Offender Networks

The following example resulted from multijurisdictional and multiagency efforts in which a ring of perpetrators, who were committing hands-on offenses via Webcam and broadcasting to each other, were identified, arrested, and prosecuted. This case highlights the extensive networks that are built and used by consumers and producers of child pornography. Additionally, emphasis is placed on the blurred boundary that exists between consumers of child pornography and hands-on offenders.

BedBugz

Agents from the North Carolina Bureau of Investigation and the FBI conducted a routine investigation in a predicated chat room and became aware of an individual operating under multiple screen names, including "sunnyfam" and "BedBugz." During undercover conversations, BedBugz sent pictures of himself and images and/or videos of child pornography.

BedBugz was identified as a middle-class, 50-year-old male from Miami, Florida. He was married to a prominent CEO and had two children. He owned his own business and was an active member in his community. By all accounts, he appeared to be a seemingly normal citizen and neighbor. However, BedBugz had joined multiple social networking sites, file-sharing networks, and predicated chat rooms to share, trade, and download images and videos of child pornography.

While search and arrest warrants were being obtained, BedBugz was observed online, via Webcam transmission, with a five-year-old female child seated on his lap. Due to the concern that the minor female child was being victimized, emergency warrants were executed.

Once apprehended, BedBugz admitted to possession and distribution of child pornography. A search of his computer revealed thousands of images and videos containing child pornography, ranging in age from infancy to preteen. During his statement to the FBI:

> BedBugz described himself as a collector of child pornography, although he knew it was wrong. BedBugz claimed that six months ago someone sent him child pornography and it peaked his interest…He admitted that he possessed both images and videos of child pornography. In response to the question of the amount of child pornography, he responded, 'too much'.

BedBugz also admitted to producing nude and posed images of his adopted 5-year-old daughter.

> He admitted that he has sent others in the chatrooms digital images of his…5-year-old daughter… He stated that one image contained his nude daughter, in a bathtub, covered in bubbles. He also admitted that one digital image of his daughter was of her nude buttocks. BedBugz admitted that he had put these digital images on the Internet for others to view.

Finally, BedBugz claimed to have engaged in "bad judgment" activities with his daughter. BedBugz admitted to having "monkey-see-monkey-do" Webcam sessions with another father/daughter duo who engaged in sexual activities on a social networking site known as Eyeball Chat. BedBugz claimed he "wasn't as bad as the fathers having sex with their children" as he was only "touching [the minor female victim] inappropriately." BedBugz identified the other father as "Trix" and was aware that the daughter was 10 years old. BedBugz admitted to directing Trix including, requesting that Trix turn the child for a better angle, adjust cameras, change the lighting, and raise the volume so he could hear. He was responsible for inducing other fathers to sexually molest and rape their children on camera for his sexual stimulation on Eyeball Chat.

Case Example 4: Offender Networks 33

One year later, BedBugz pleaded guilty to all charges and was subsequently sentenced to a prison term of 23 years for his crimes.

Trix

"Trix" was identified as a 54-year-old Caucasian male. He lived with his "life partner," a single mother with two daughters, ages 8 and 10 years old. Images of Trix with the 10-year-old female victim were recovered from BedBugz's computer. Search and arrest warrants were executed for Trix's residence. A search of Trix's computer revealed no child pornography; however, Trix openly admitted to using a "shredder" to eliminate all traces of pornography.

Upon arrest, Trix also admitted to sexually abusing both of the minor females that he had access to and engaging in Webcam sessions with other father/daughters. He engaged in sexual activity with the minor female victims for the other members of the group through the use of a Webcam, and in exchange, the other members would engage in sexual activity with their female victims on Webcam for Trix's observation. During his statement to the FBI, Trix was asked,

> at what age [the minor female victim] would not be sexually attractive to him; Trix replied that he believed he would begin having "consensual sex" with [the minor female victim] when she turned 13 or 14 and he believed their sexual relationship would continue indefinitely.

Trix also claimed that he permitted another adult male to engage in sexual activity with the minor female victim on multiple occasions. Finally, Trix admitted to engaging in Webcam sessions with other fathers including, "sunnyfam" (BedBugz, above), "Redbed," and "Samson." Trix consented for federal agents to assume the screen name "Trix". Trix pleaded guilty to two counts of production of child pornography and two counts of transportation of child pornography and was subsequently sentenced to a prison term of 54 years.

Samson

Under the assumed identity of "Trix," the FBI identified Samson as a Caucasian male and previously convicted sex offender from Front Royal, Virginia. Trix (above) identified conversations with Samson, in which he planned to rape his teenage daughter when his pregnant wife went to the hospital to deliver their baby.

A search warrant was executed for Samson's residence. Samson admitted to sexually abusing at least three minor female children, the youngest of which was one week old at the onset of abuse. Authorities identified and rescued all three minor female children. Samson was convicted of multiple crimes involving sexual exploitation of children. He was sentenced to a prison term of life. However, Samson committed suicide in prison, while awaiting his final sentencing.

Redbed

Under the assumed identity of "Trix," the FBI was able to identify Redbed. It was known that.

> Redbed sent Trix (above) several jpeg images of his naked daughter with "use me" written on the girl...[and] said he also has a 5 or 6-year-old daughter he has molested...Redbed referred to his 7-year-old daughter as "my slut" and he told Trix he had physically raped and anally penetrated the girl. Trix observed an Eyeball Chat webcast from Redbed's home computer wherein Redbed's daughter performed oral sex on him.

Upon arrest, Redbed consented for the FBI to assume the screen name "Redbed." Redbed provided information on at least four other screen names that were members of their Webcam group including, "Branibabe," "Ashygirl," "Modelmaker," and "KoCtuk." Each screen name was identified, arrested, and prosecuted. Two female children were identified and rescued from Redbed's abuse. Redbed pleaded guilty on charges of transportation of a minor and possession of child pornography. He was subsequently sentenced to a prison term of 13 years and 6 months.

Overall, federal, and state agents identified and rescued 12 children that were being sexually exploited over the Internet by their guardians. A total of nine hands-on offenders were identified and arrested. Finally, federal agents were able to identify three new child pornography series in the Child Victim Identification Program (CVIP) database at the National Center for Missing and Exploited Children.[1]

---

[1] The Child Victim Identification Program (CVIP) database at the National Center for Missing and Exploited Children is key in assisting the prosecution of pornography cases across the country. In some venues, the database has been used to determine that the images of victims have traveled in interstate commerce (i.e., the Internet) or affected interstate commerce in some manner (i.e., sale or trade). By demonstrating that the identified victim is located in one state/country and that the possessor/distributor is located in another state, that element of the crime has been met. In addition, law enforcement has utilized the database to confirm the ages and identities of known victims or to enter newly identified victims. The ability to store and track images of victims across the country has assisted law enforcement in the identification, location, and deliverance of victims of child pornography.

Chapter 7
Sex Tourism

Child sex tourism is a lucrative and global industry (Todres 1999). Wonders and Michalowski (2001) carefully defined sex tourism as "the convergence between prostitution and tourism, [it] links the global and the local and draws attention to both the production and consumption of sexual services" (p. 545). Sex tourism includes trips facilitated by the tourism sector for the explicit purpose of engaging in commercial sexual relationships with residents. Sexual offenders use the structures of the tourism industry to expedite travel and facilitate crime. Sex tourism is rooted in the long-standing problem of international child prostitution. However, sex tourism is unique in that it involves the transport of the offender rather than the transport of the victim. Consequently, sex tourism has offered American citizens an opportunity to engage in illicit sexual activities with marginalized populations beyond the threat of prosecution because different legislative bodies rule foreign countries. Therefore, the lower ages of consent, the legalization of prostitution, and the absence of extradition laws in foreign countries can make sex tourism an appealing option for American sexual offenders.

The US and other source/sending countries play a substantial role in the perpetuation of sex tourism (Li 1995). Tourists feed the sex tourism industry by continuing the demand for sexually available children. Unlike previously discussed CSEC crimes, the actual exploitation and fiscal exchange occurs in foreign countries with foreign-born children. Offenders originate in another country and then the destination country supplies the victims and acts as the location of the actual abuse (US Department of Justice 2007). Regardless of the actual locations of exploitation, sex tourism remains a domestic concern as American citizens continue to travel abroad to engage in illicit acts with minors.

Sex tourists often target less-developed countries (US Department of Justice, 2007). Central and South America have recently become prime locations for pedophiles or opportunists seeking underage exploits (Walters and Davis 2011). Todres (1999) identified the US as a primary "supplier of sex tourists to Central America" (p. 3–4). The appeal of underdeveloped nations is the anonymity and refuge offered to sexual offenders that permits them to continue offending. Additionally, Destination countries such as Asia, Central, or South America may have local legislation and extradition laws in place; however, these laws may be loosely enforced or served with more lenient penalties compared to the US (Steinman 2002). Governments and officials may further exacerbate the problem by rarely enforcing the laws resulting in continued exploitation. Finally, corrupt law enforcement agencies may also encourage further exploitation. For example, one incident recounted "an illegal operation where foreigners sexually exploit children, [and] a high ranking police official [was] inside the building helping the American owner escape off the back wall" (Steinman 2002, p. 67). The demand for sexually available youth and the negligence of official agencies has permitted the exploitation of foreign children by domestic tourists to develop into an insidious and pervasive problem.

Victims of sex tourism are characterized by the same vulnerability factors as other CSEC victims. Lack of education, poverty, disintegrated or neglectful families, and physical or sexual abuse are common risk factors for children coerced into sex tourism (Berkman 1996; Steinman 2002). Additionally, political and economic upheaval contributes to the rising problem of sex tourism. Specifically, an essential feature of sex tourism is the extent to which impoverished and developing countries look to tourism as a potentially profitable source of income and possible reprieve from economic pressures (Robinson 1997). Consequently, the increased promotion of tourism correlates with the influx of perpetrators wishing to exploit a marginalized population: children.

Offender Characteristics

Similar to other consumers of child sexual exploitation, few data exist to develop a concrete profile of a sex tourist. Additionally, the variability among consumers makes it nearly impossible to generate a consensus regarding shared features of sex tourists. However, researchers tend to agree that sex tourists are commonly males between the ages of 28 and 68, most often American, European, or Asian in origin (Li 1995; Robinson 1997; Thomas and Matthews 2006). The individual who engages in sex tourism may be a convicted sexual offender and pedophile, or they may be seemingly normal educators, servicemen, or higher professional such as doctors and lawyers (Steinman 2002).

Sex tourists are divided into two general categories, based on their motivations and interests: (1) preferential abusers, or (2) situational abusers (Lanning 2001; Walters and Davis 2011).[1] Preferential abusers include pedophiles who have clearly defined sexual preferences for children and travel internationally in order to satisfy their sexual drive. The situational abuser, on the other hand, does not repeatedly engage in sexual relations with children. This individual most likely does not travel with the intent of engaging in commercialized sex with a minor but does so

---

[1] See page 27 for definitions.

when the opportunity is presented (Walters and Davis 2011). The situational abuser may be drawn to the anonymity offered by a foreign land and partake in the opportunity to expand sexual horizons, void of social taboos, and engage in sex with a minor (Steinman 2002).

The passing of the Sexual Offender Act of 1994 (i.e., Megan's Law) in the US has acted as a catalyst for shifting the sex tourism industry across international borders, particularly to Latin America (Steinman 2002). Since 1994, mandatory registration and community notifications have restricted the domestic movements of child sexual offenders. As a result, perpetrators take advantage of the opportunity to satiate sexual appetites by traveling outside American borders in search of children to exploit. Take, for example, the man who travels across the US-Mexican border on repeated occasions in search of young, male Mexican prostitutes. This perpetrator likely chooses Latin America as the proximity to the US offers the daily accessibility of inexpensive, underage prostitutes (Walters and Davis 2011).

According to the US Department of Justice (2011), sex tourists resort to distorted rationalizations to justify their exploits:

> Some perpetrators rationalize their sexual encounters with children with the idea that they are helping the children financially better themselves and their families. Paying a child for his or her services allows a tourist to avoid guilt by convincing himself he is helping the child and the child's family to escape economic hardship. Others try to justify their behavior by reasoning that children in foreign countries are less "sexually inhibited," and through the belief that their destination country does not have the same social taboos against having sex with children (p. 1).

Regardless of justifications for their actions, "sex tourists are no different than child molesters and other sex offenders" (Walters and Davis 2011, p. 9).

Mechanism of Sex Tourism

Industry is the driving force behind sex tourism. Similar to other CSEC crimes, the child is seen as a sexual commodity. The tourist provides the consumer demand for which the agent fulfills the demand with human goods. Unfortunately, there is seemingly no end to this perverse economic pattern in that, as long as there is a demand for sexually available youth, there will be a supply of children to exploit.

Foreign youth prostitutes satisfy multiple needs for offenders. For example, the young age and physical immaturity can satisfy an offender's virgin fantasy or pedophilic urges (Li 1995). Offenders also solicit children for sex under the misconception that a child will be less likely to be infected by HIV (Berkman 1996). However, research shows that prostituted children are more likely than adult prostitutes to carry HIV as well as other sexually transmitted diseases (Fraley 2012).

Similar to the mechanism of prostitution, sex tourism includes both procurers and facilitators (Robinson 1997). Procurers, or pimps, are the individuals who make child sex tourism a profitable industry; they provide the service in response to the demand. Facilitators, however, are individuals who "expedite the victimization process" and are not directly involved in the sexually exploitative transaction. In the case of sex tourism, facilitators include the sex tour travel agent/agency, permissible hotel owners, or the parents who sell their child into prostitution (Robinson 1997).

Sex tours can be booked and planned in a manner similar to typical family vacations. Tourists can independently plan their vacations via the Internet, or sex tours can be organized by travel agencies (Li 1995). At one point, there were over 25 known companies operating in the US that offered sex tours (Todres 1999). Sex tourism newsletters and brochures advertise adventures available to persons who are intent on having sex with minors (Berkman 1996). For example, "The Erotic Traveler," formally known as the "Asia Files," is a newsletter that provides information on traveling and sexual exploits in both Asia and Latin America (Steinman 2002). Destinations are primarily to developing regions such as Thailand, the Philippines, or Latin America; "the price of a typical ten-day or two-week tour ranges from US $1,800 to 2,500 per person and includes round-trip airfare… hotel accommodations, ground transportation, a local guide, and introductions to lady companions throughout [the] stay as desired" (Todres 1999, p. 4).

Case Example 5: The Preferential Sexual Tourist

Raul

Raul was a 47-year-old, married, Hispanic male who held a trusted position as the butler for a government official. Raul had no prior arrest record; however, he had a history of extensive marijuana use. It is unknown if Raul engaged in sexual tourism or other sexual offenses prior to this point; however, at the time of his arrest, Raul expressed an interest in hands-on offending.

As previously stated, sexual tours are often publicly advertised in local travel publications and on the Internet. Raul contacted one of these online travel agency that advertised travel to an exotic location, access to local activities, and selection of sexual companions. His request for a sexual companion included "…young… very young…fourteen, sixteen is good." Raul also strategized his vacation to coincide with his wife's absence from the country.

His employer gave a statement to police acknowledging that approximately three weeks prior to his arrest; Raul had requested time off to visit an ailing family member:

> [Raul] advised [his employer] that he was going to New York to visit his sick mother… [He then] advised that his travel plans had changed. Raul told [his employer] he would be going to Atlanta, Georgia as his mother had relocated there to be with [his] sister while she was recovering from her illness.

Federal agents apprehended Raul at the airport. While in custody, Raul continued to deny his intent to engage in sexual activities with a minor. He was adamant that

Case Example 5: The Preferential Sexual Tourist   39

he requested only adult escorts and agreed to minors only after being misled by the travel agent. Raul admitted that he had thought about [engaging in sex with a minor] but was afraid and "did not want a big hassle." Similarly, Raul denied his explicit request for a 14- to 16-year-old sexual companion. However, upon hearing the portion of his recorded conversation in which he made this request, he responded, "wow" and continued to insist he was not going to engage in sex with a minor.

Raul was found guilty on charges of enticement and commercial sex tourism. He was subsequently sentenced to a prison term of 10 years.

Case Example 6: The Repeat Tourist

Richard

Richard was a 57-year-old Caucasian male who had separated from his wife. He owned his own lumber business in New York and was a self-proclaimed "loner." Richard had a prior criminal history including several arrests for failure to pay child support, burglary, unlawfully growing cannabis, and unauthorized use of a vehicle. Additionally, at 21 years of age, Richard engaged in illicit sexual activity with an unidentified, 16-year-old female. Unfortunately, no charges were filed against Richard for this prior sexual offense.

Richard had a long pattern of foreign travel to engage in sexual activities. He reported that he had previously booked a trip to Thailand through a travel agency that provided sexual companions. Although Richard's wife denied knowledge of Richard's illegal activities, she disclosed to law enforcement that Richard had traveled to Mexico on numerous occasions for what she assumed was to engage in sex:

> During January/February of 2005, [Richard] drove their RV [recreational vehicle] to the Southwestern border of the U.S. and stayed for approximately two months. [She] did not accompany him on this trip. She stated that he would park the RV very near the border and frequently walk[ed] over into Juarez, Mexico. She did not know for sure what he was doing in Juarez; however, she assumed it had something to do with sex.

In reference to his travels across the US–Mexico border, Richard admitted.

> There was a girl in Mexico I would have brought back you know and….it was just ["too take out"] much a freaking hassle.

Richard blamed his deviant sexual behavior on his life circumstances. His business was doing poorly due to the decline of the housing market. He was also in the midst of a tumultuous divorce. Richard claimed he had not engaged in sexual relations with his wife for a number of years and was driven to extramarital affairs. Also, his wife forced Richard to live in the recreation vehicle located on the same property as the primary residence.

Richard saw his overseas trip as an opportunity to "get drunk and get laid." He booked an "all-inclusive vacation" which included travel to an exotic location, local activities, and a companion. Richard selected his choice of companion based on the gender, age, and the preferred sexual acts. He paid approximately $2,000 for international airfare, meals, hotel accommodations, tourist attractions, and the sexual services of a companion. Richard explicitly requested underage females between the ages of 14 and 15 years as his sexual companions, stating:

> Yeah, I'd like to try a younger one then of course something a little more mature.

When later asked his reasons for requesting a 14–15-year-old, Richard responded "[I] didn't know why, but [I] decided to try it."

Richard was intercepted by federal agents at the airport. He was charged with traveling in interstate commerce for sex traveling across state lines, sexual tourism, and enticement. He pleaded guilty to one count of traveling in foreign commerce to engage in sexual activity with a minor. As a result of his cooperation with authorities, Richard was subsequently sentenced to five days in jail with time served, five years of supervised release, a $100 fine, and mandatory registration as a sex offender.

The preceding case examples reflect the nature of the child sex tourism industry. Offenders are primarily men who may be travelers, but who take advantage of a given opportunity. They are most often pedophiles, preferentially attracted to minors. They often justify their exploits as benevolent actions of humanitarianism; however, the unfortunate reality is that, regardless of their marginalized existence, children sexually exploited by foreign travelers suffer the same ill effects as domestic, sexually exploited youth.

Chapter 8
Sex Traveler/Enticer

Although not highly researched, law enforcement recognizes the "traveler/enticer" as a specific type of sexual offender which warrants classification as a form of commercialized sexual exploitation. Legally, the sex traveler/enticer is identified as an offender who "travels in interstate or foreign commerce for the purpose of engaging in any illicit sexual conduct with another person" [18 USC § 2423(b)] more specifically using "interstate commerce or foreign commerce…to knowingly persuade, induce, or entice a minor to engage in… any illegal sexual activity [18 § U.S.C. 2422(a)]." Sex tourism and traveling may appear to be related offenses; however, there are differences between them. Both offenses entail the travel of one individual to the other with the purpose of engaging in sexual contact. Victims of sex tourism are exploited in foreign countries whereas travelers exploit minors within the US. Most important and unique to sex traveling, is the component of enticement. Enticement includes the use of any interstate or intrastate facility, such as the Internet, cellular telephones, postal services, or text messages, to facilitate the deception of a minor with the intent of engaging in illicit sexual activity.

The Internet has offered travelers the expediency and ease of online offending. It has also increased an offender's accessibility to vulnerable youth. For example, research gathered from the National Center for Missing and Exploited Children indicated that one in five children between the ages of 10 and 17 were sexually solicited over the Internet (Finkelhor et al., 2000). Additionally, one in 33 children received some form of an aggressive solicitation that included sending them regular mail, money, or gifts, using the telephone to contact them, or the solicitor asking to meet somewhere (Medaris and Girouard 2002).

Hernandez (2000) found additional support for the prevalence of traveling among CSEC offenders. This investigation assessed incidence rates of contact crimes among inmates arrested solely on charges of possession and/or distribution of child pornography. Participants were organized into three groups based on correlating crimes: (1) the "Child Pornography/Traveler" group, (2) the "Contact Sexual Offender" group, and (3) the "Other" group which included offenders convicted of nonsexual crimes. The largest of the preceding groups was the "Child Pornography/Traveler" group. It included 62 inmates who were convicted of various pornography and traveling offenses including luring a child and/or traveling across state lines with the intent of sexually abusing a child. The "Child Pornography/Traveler" group was also identified as having the highest incidence of hands-on offenses (an average of 30.5 per offender) when compared with the other offender groups.

Offender Characteristics

To our knowledge, there is no research that identifies demographic characteristics specific to travelers. However, federally informed data have identified middle-aged, Caucasian males as the primary offenders. They can vary in level of education, occupation, and socioeconomic status. Travelers may or may not collect child pornography as many are not interested in mere fantasy; rather, their goal is the hands-on victimization of a minor. Law enforcement experience suggests that travelers tend to be preferential offenders who target minors to engage in illicit sexual activity. Preferential travelers may demonstrate a preference for one gender within a specific age group or they may victimize children across gender and age groups (Lanning 2001). Additionally, travelers may also be situational offenders. Similar to other CSEC offenders, situational travelers engage in illicit sexual activity with minors through opportunity or convenience.

Specific trends have been identified based purely on a review of various federal traveling cases. First, travelers typically have some knowledge and be technologically savvy to navigate through the Internet, chat rooms, and social networking sites. Second, they must need the resources to fund their travel and/or to entice their victims. Therefore, they may be employed or have other means of securing funds. Finally, certain characteristic elements may be common among travelers. For example, they appear to have antisocial features including skill at manipulating others. Further, they may present as emotionally immature adults who socialize more comfortably with younger age groups.

Mechanism of Sex Traveling

Travelers will use online sources, including chat rooms and social networking sites, to target confused, neglected, or troubled youth. Like many CSEC victims, travelers "[prey] on child victims who are experiencing other challenges in their lives, such as learning disabilities, a fractured family life, or a period of depression, exacerbated by the already-complex insecurities of preteen years, [Travelers]…have an uncanny ability to identify fragile victims" (Kendall and Funk 2012, p. 24).

The ultimate goal of the traveler is to gain the trust of and subsequent access to, a minor. Therefore, similar to other forms of commercialized exploitation, they will use various techniques to groom their victims. For example, they may send the victim gifts, money, or provide emotional support. They may also send the victim child pornography in an attempt to "break down inhibitions and validate sex between children and adults" (Medaris and Girouard 2002, p. 2). In many cases, a traveler's grooming process is scrupulous and time-consuming. For example, a traveler may take several weeks to several months to learn about his victim's interests, family, friends, and weaknesses. Gifts are used to stimulate the victim's interests and ultimately earn the offender trust and access. In addition, travelers may develop alternate facades by which to dupe their victims and "depending on the fictitious persona the offender has created for his victim(s), communication with the victims may be necessary throughout the day in the form of text messages, chats, and emails" (Kendall and Funk 2001, p. 24).

Once the traveler has earned the victim's trust, he will lure or persuade the victim to meet him. Importantly, traveling/enticement offenses include luring a minor to a designated location or persuading a minor to consent for the offender to meet them. For example, the traveler may convince the victim to meet him in a public location, such as at a shopping mall or cinema. He may also persuade the victim to allow him to come to one of their common locations such as their house or school. Further, traveling crimes can occur within one block to thousands of miles between the victim and offender. Similarly, the traveler may entice and victimize multiple victims simultaneously or, they may continue to abuse one victim on multiple occasions.

Case Example 7: The Enticement/Grooming Process of a Traveler

Miguel, a 15-year-old Mexican immigrant, lived with his single mother and one sibling. He was an introverted boy who was known for being a good student and hard worker. He had no history of delinquency, drug use, or behavioral problems. As an adolescent in a foreign country and without a father, Miguel struggled to "fit in." Moreover, Miguel had recently begun to question his sexuality.

Miguel entered online chartrooms in search of answers, support, and friendship. In 2008, he chatted with an adult, male who he met online identified as David. David was a 38-year-old, Hispanic male with no prior criminal record. Over the course of five months, David groomed Miguel by sending him gifts, love letters, and nude pictures of himself. He capitalized on Miguel's insecurity and curiosity. In gaining the support and trust of his victim, David had become an important fixture in his life and had carefully gained emotional control over the youth.

Within a few months, David arranged to meet Miguel. He drove over 1,300 miles from Florida to Texas. David picked Miguel up from school and drove him to a nearby hotel where he engaged in illegal sexual conduct with the minor. He then took pornographic photos of Miguel for his personal use. Approximately three months later, David made the trip again to engage in illegal sexual conduct with Miguel.

During this second trip, "Miguel's" mother became suspicious of his behavior when she realized that he had been with David. She contacted the local police and had her son call David asking him to return. When David returned to see Miguel, awaiting authorities took David into custody for the sexual assault that had occurred earlier that day. David confessed to engaging in sexual activity with Miguel and was charged with traveling, the production of child pornography, and enticement of a minor to engage in illegal sexual conduct. David was convicted and sentenced to a prison term of 5 years. Upon the completion of his prison term, David will be deported to his home country in Central America.

Case Example 8: Luring Behaviors of a Traveler

In February 2001, an undercover law enforcement officer conducted a routine investigation in an online chat room, "Family Fun." An individual identified as K. Jackson began chatting and exchanging images of child pornography with the undercover. Over time, Jackson expressed an interest in engaging in sexual activity with the undercover's 12-year-old son. He stated that he had been "hunting and hunting for something like this."

Jackson was identified as a 36-year-old, Caucasian male. He was open about his sexual preference, suffered from a severe medical condition, and lived with his life partner, M. Wilson. In February of 2001, Jackson traveled to a hotel in Florida, to engage in the sexual encounter with the undercover's 12-year-old boy. When he arrived at the designated meeting, law enforcement arrested and charged him with child exploitation and traveling with the intent to engage in sexual activity with a minor. A search of his vehicle revealed sexual paraphernalia, a teddy bear, Viagra, and crystal methamphetamines. The state court admitted Jackson to conditions of pretrial release which included abstaining from Internet usage. However, he was later found guilty of violating conditions of his pretrial release. A federal search warrant of Jackson's residence was executed, resulting in the seizure of computers containing child pornography and illicit drugs. On-scene detectives and federal agents observed ongoing chats that included discussions of having sex with infants and child pornography. Jackson, while handcuffed, ran from law enforcement into his room and attempted to destroy the computer by hitting his head against it in an attempt to knock it to the ground. Both Jackson and police officers sustained injuries. Jackson was prosecuted.

During Jackson's bond hearing and prior to the sentencing, Wilson threatened witnesses and the testifying FBI Special Agent. At the time of his arrest for these allegations, Wilson was wearing a fanny pack with a loaded 9-mm pistol. Wilson spent 60 days in jail and then entered a guilty plea in exchange for a reduced charge. In 2003, Jackson completed his prison term. He was sentenced to a prison term of 10 years and 8 months followed by three years supervised release. He was released back to the residence that he shared with Wilson. Computers were permitted into the residence on Wilson's assertion that they were necessary for his modeling and acting career. At the time of Wilson's release, Jackson's probation officer noted Wilson's overt hostility toward law enforcement.

Several years later, the same undercover law enforcement officer was conducting a routine investigation in an online chat room. During the investigation, he encountered an individual who sent images containing child pornography and expressed an interest in meeting children to engage in sexual intercourse. This individual was identified as Jackson, operating under a different screen name than his prior arrest. Search and arrest warrants were executed for Jackson in July of 2004.

While in state custody, recorded jail calls between Wilson and Jackson revealed Jackson soliciting Wilson to "take care" of witnesses. Additionally, recorded calls revealed information that caused authorities to suspect that additional child pornography was located in the garage of the Wilson/Jackson residence. Following Jackson's arrest, law enforcement returned to the Wilson residence with a federal search warrant for the child pornography and a federal arrest warrant for Wilson for witness tampering/conspiracy. A task force composed of police officers and federal agents were assembled to arrest Wilson at his residence. As police entered the residence, Wilson opened fire from a carefully chosen vantage point. He shot and killed a Sheriff's Deputy and severely injured another. After several minutes, Wilson emerged from the residence, unarmed, and surrendered. A search of the house revealed an arsenal of weapons in strategic locations throughout the residence. Additionally, child pornography and incriminating communications between Wilson and Jackson were confiscated.

Letters between Wilson and Jackson illustrate Wilson's growing hostility toward law enforcement:

> ...have been becoming a mean and bitter person. I have been have problems with my anger lately. It seem[s] my anger has been [a] trigger. I guess the way I deal with stress is to internalize it, and I feel like a boiling teapot... and I get so angry I want to kill every cop I see. I will never stop hating cops for the rest of my life. I will devote my life attacking the police and avenging you for all they have done.

Additionally, writings from Wilson during his participation in a local university psychological study demonstrate his intent against law enforcement:

> I know that picking fight with cops is insane but I need to vent my rage over an injustice. I guess in many way[s] this is the edge of madness. I have several weapon[s] just laying around in case one of the nut jobs actually show up.

In September 2005, Jackson pleaded guilty to his charges and was subsequently sentenced to a prison term of 24 years and 5 months. After a 10-week federal trial, Wilson was found guilty for the premeditated murder of a federal law enforcement officer and the attempted murder of others. He was sentenced to serve a prison term of three consecutive life sentences.

Chapter 9
CSEC Legislation

After exploring the different forms and mechanisms of commercial sexual exploitation of children (CSEC), it is important to review the legal practices and legislation used to prosecute CSEC offenders. The first portion of the legislation section will review pertinent history, while the second section will emphasize currently used federal statutes and provisions.

Legislative History

Children are an undeniably at-risk population. The immaturity and subsequent inability to consent to sexual acts has provoked the international community to create standards that protect the rights of children. More specifically, the United Nations Convention on the Rights of the Child developed five articles that explicitly detail the manner in which children are protected from coercion into prostitution under international doctrine (Table 9.1).

While international law provides suggestions and guidance to law enforcement internationally, they are not enforceable in the same manner that State and Federal laws are enforced. Therefore, a careful review of the history of legislative change regarding the rights of children is necessary. In 2000, the Trafficking Victims Prevention Act (TVPA) was introduced and allotted over $95 million for anti-trafficking law enforcement and assistance programs. Also included in the law were regulations for severe punishments, such as life in prison and severe economic sanctions for those convicted of human trafficking. In both 2003 and 2005, the reauthorizations of TVPA added more specific provisions for the prosecution of human trafficking crimes. For example, the American legal system was authorized to prosecute offenses committed overseas by government employees or contractors. The FBI was also given jurisdiction to investigate severe forms of trafficking both domestically and internationally. And finally, the provisions included increased prevention services.

Table 9.1 Articles protecting children from coercion into prostitution under international doctrine United Nations Convention on the Rights of the Child

Article 19:	"States parties shall take all appropriate legislative, administrative, social and educational measures to protect the child from all forms of physical or mental violence, injury or abuse, neglect or negligent treatment, maltreatment or exploitation, including sexual abuse, while in the care of parent(s), legal guardian(s) or any other person who has the care of the child" (p. 5)
Article 32:	"States Parties recognize the right of the child to be protected from economic exploitation and from performing any work that is likely to be hazardous or to interfere with the child's education, or to be harmful to the child's health or physical, mental, spiritual, moral or social development" (p. 9)
Article 34:	"States Parties undertake to protect the child from all forms of sexual exploitation and sexual abuse. For these purposes, States Parties shall in particular take all appropriate national, bilateral and multilateral measures to prevent: (a) The inducement or coercion of a child to engage in any unlawful sexual activity; (b) The exploitative use of children in prostitution or other unlawful sexual practices; (c) The exploitative use of children in pornographic performances and materials" (p. 10)
Article 36:	"States Parties shall protect the child against all other forms of exploitation prejudicial to any aspects of the child's welfare" (p. 10)
Article 39:	"States Parties shall take all appropriate measures to promote physical and psychological recovery and social reintegration of a child victim of: any form of neglect, exploitation, or abuse; torture or any other form of cruel, inhuman or degrading treatment or punishment; or armed conflicts. Such recovery and reintegration shall take place in an environment which fosters the health, self-respect and dignity of the child" (p. 11)

Additionally, the William Wilberforce Trafficking Victims Protection Reauthorization Act of 2008 strengthened Federal efforts to fight international and domestic trafficking. Section 1589 allows for "prosecution under subsection (a)(1) in which the defendant had a reasonable opportunity to observe the person so recruited, enticed, harbored, transported, provided, obtained or maintained, the Government need not prove that the defendant knew that the person had not attained the age of 18 years" (p. 26). From the Reauthorization Act, prosecutors no longer have the burden of proof that the offender was cognizant of the minor status of the child. It also criminalized all acts of pimping and pandering even without proof of force, fraud, coercion, or the victim's age (p. 40). Importantly, the new statutes do not require that trafficking involve coercion when the victim is a child, nor does it mandate that the child must cross international or state borders to be considered trafficked. In other words, the Protection Reauthorization Act of 2008 effectively made the movement of children for the purposes of exploitation a Federal crime.

Regarding child pornography, the Communication Decency Act (CDA) and Child Pornography Prevention Act (CPPA) were passed by Congress in 1996. The CDA was the first Federal legislation to confront the problem of child pornography. The CDA made it illegal to distribute obscene or indecent material via the Internet. However, the ambiguity of the statute was effectively publicized by

Reno v. American Civil Liberties Union (Graham 2000). Moreover, the legislation does not use language specifically related to child pornography. Despite seemingly weak applications of the CDA to child pornography cases, prosecutors may cite the legislation in an effort to prosecute child pornographers.

In contrast, the CPPA explicitly addresses child pornography. The CPPA criminalizes "any visual depiction, including any photograph, film, video, picture, or computer-generated image or picture that is, or appears to be, of a minor engaging in sexually explicit conduct" (Section 8, paragraph a). Second, the CPPA prohibits "any sexually explicit image that was advertised, promoted, presented, described, or distributed in such a manner that conveys the impression of a minor engaging in sexually explicit conduct" (Section 8, paragraph b). The CPAA thus criminalizes the possession and distribution of pornographic images depicting minors. Consequently, the CPAA is a more effective piece of legislation to prosecute offenders and eliminate pornographic exploitation of children.

Current Federal Laws Used to Prosecute CSEC Offenders

This section will review each individual statute used to prosecute offenders. However, it is important to remember that with the distinctive overlap of CSEC crimes, many offenders are charged with multiple counts.

Child trafficking, traveling, enticement, and prostitution are prosecuted under various statutes. First, regarding traveling cases, Title 18 United States Code § 2422(a) prohibits anyone from luring a child under 18 years of age by knowingly persuading, inducing, enticing, or coercing any person to travel in interstate or foreign commerce to engage in prostitution or sexual activity that constitutes a criminal offense. This statute is used when offenders manipulate children to travel for the purposes of exploitation. Enticement is prosecuted under 18 USC § 2422(b); 18 USC § 2422(b) prohibits a person from using the mail or any other means of interstate commerce, including a computer, to knowingly persuade, induce, entice, or coerce a minor to engage in prostitution or any illegal sexual activity. This offense is punishable by up to 20 years imprisonment.

When offenders lure victims to a designated meeting location and subsequently transport that victim for the purposes of exploitation, they are charged with 18 USC § 2423(a). More specifically, this statute prohibits any person from transporting a child under 18 years of age in interstate commerce with the intent that the child engage in prostitution or any other criminal sexual activity. A violation of 18 USC § 2423(a) has a minimum sentence of 10 years and a maximum of life imprisonment. Conversely, 18 USC § 2423(b) is applied when offenders travel to meet children. It makes it a Federal crime to travel in interstate or foreign commerce for the purpose of engaging in any illicit sexual conduct with another person. This violation is punishable by up to 30 years imprisonment. A Federal law prohibits the recruitment, enticement, harboring, or transportation of a minor, in or affecting interstate or foreign commerce, knowing that the minor will be caused to engage in commercial sex act., in violation of 18 USC § 1591. Such violations are punishable by a minimum of 15 years and a maximum of life imprisonment if the child is under 14 years of age. If the child is 14 or older, the minimum mandatory sentence is 10 years up to life. Finally, offenders can be charged with selling or buying children under 18 USC § 225, punishable by a minimum mandatory sentence of 30 years up to life in prison.

Most frequently, the statute called upon to prosecute pornography offenders is Title 18 US Code, Chapter 110—Sexual Exploitation and Other Abuse of Children and Chapter 117—Transportation for Illegal Sexual Activity and Related Crimes. In child pornography cases, offenders can be prosecuted as possessors, recipients, distributors, or producers. These crimes are prosecuted under 18 USC §§ 2251, 2252, 2252A, respectively. Simple possession of child pornography is punishable by up to 10 years in prison under 18 USC § 2252 (a) (4) (B) and 2252 (a) (5) (B). Further, receipt, transportation, or distribution of child pornography is punishable under 18 USC §§ 2252 (a) and 2252A (a) (1) and (2) with a minimum penalty of 5 years and no more than 20 years. Finally, production and advertising of child pornography is punishable by a minimum mandatory sentence of 15 years and a maximum of 30 years imprisonment under 18 USC §§ 2251 and 2260 (a).

Finally, law enforcement officials use additional statutes to prosecute the ancillary crimes that occur in the process of CSEC. These include the transfer of obscene material to minors (18 USC § 1470), punishable by up to 10 years, the aggravated sexual abuse of a child (18 USC § 2250) punishable by up to life imprisonment, and the failure to register as a sex offender (18 USC § 2250), punishable by up to 10 years. Further, if offenders do not forfeit the property they acquired as a result of these illegal activities, they can face criminal forfeiture under 18 USC § 2253. Also, Federal law can require a defendant to pay restitution to the child victim in terms of medical or psychological services, necessary transportation, child care expenses, temporary housing, lost income, attorney's fees, and other losses suffered due to the crime. These victim rights are protected under 18 USC § 2259.

Chapter 10
Conclusion

Commercial sexual exploitation of children (CSEC) is the sexual exploitation of children for personal or monetary gain. Forms of CSEC include child trafficking, child pornography, child prostitution, child sex tourism, and child sex traveling. CSEC is maintained through the supply and demand of children to sexually exploit. The impact of CSEC can be felt both internationally and nationally. In an effort to end the exploitation of children and aid CSEC victims, we have provided professionals with clarified distinctions between various forms of commercialized exploitation, insight into mechanisms of CSEC, and acknowledged trends in typology of victims and offenders. We have further provided primary source case studies to exemplify particularly salient characteristics of both victims and offenders.

The information provided in this review is not exhaustive. Other forms of child exploitation include child laundering, child labor, and kidnapping. Unfortunately, limited research exists in reference to these forms of exploitation. Unlike previously discussed forms of exploitation, these crimes are not inherently commercial or sexual in nature; however, forms of child exploitation do not occur in mutual exclusion (Bump and Duncan 2003; Kern 2000).

Similar to prostitution and pornography, illegal adoptions and "black market babies" are a form of child exploitation in which a child is commodified. Victims are assumed to be supplied from impoverished countries to more developed countries, such as the US, Canada, and Europe (Kapstein 2003; Smolin 2006). The process of child laundering includes three steps: (1) obtaining the child through abduction or parental sale to "baby brokers," (2) falsification of the child's paperwork, and (3) processing the child as an "orphan" through the intercountry adoption system (Smolin 2006, 2007). The root of the child laundering problem is the illegal acquisition of these children. These victims are stripped from or sold by their biological families and are international transplanted. Equally victimized are "adoptees" that have unknowingly supported black market crime and the exploitation of children.

Child labor is another form of child exploitation. Goddard and White (1982) defined child labor as "illegal; universally underpaid and often unpaid; often not conceived of as 'labour' at all but disguised as some form of training, helping, etc." (p. 466). The Bureau of International Labor, US Department of Labor (1994) identified that 95 % of all child laborers were employed in developing countries. The extent to which exploitative child labor is recognized as an international problem relates to the minimal amount of research dedicated to address child labor as a domestic problem. In the US, exploitation of child labor has been known to be present in the sweatshops of New York's Chinatown and Garment District and in the citrus groves of Florida and California (Moran 1993). However, few data exist to estimate the actual impact of domestic labor exploitation or identify victims of child labor.

Finally, kidnapping is a form of child exploitation that has recently regained public concern due to the infamous cases such as Jaycee Dugard and Elizabeth Smart (Kendall and Funk 2012). Such cases have re-contextualized kidnapping as a form of child sexual exploitation. Child kidnapping is not inherently commercial, however. Perpetrators may utilize other forms of CSEC, such as "pimping out" a captive child or producing pornographic images, resulting in commercialized exploitation. Despite the more recent publicity, there is little empirical research that has identified trends in mechanisms or motives specific to kidnapping and exploitation of children. More importantly, Jaycee and Elizabeth were from middle-class, well-adjusted families and suffered no previous abuse, unlike the traumatic histories common among CSEC victims. Future research should explore the disparity between kidnapping and other CSEC crimes by examining the modus operandi, targeted victims, and offender characteristics.

The actual impact of CSEC is unknown; however, CSEC has proven to be a ubiquitous crime that includes various forms of exploitation, with domestic and international concerns. Offenders target marginalized, disenfranchised, and vulnerable youth for personal and/or financial gain. Victims are intellectually, physically, and socially disadvantaged, thus minimizing their ability to escape their abuse. Consequently, young victims of commercialized sexual exploitation are entrenched in a system of manipulation, crime, and abuse. Victims who escape are perpetually re-traumatized by the physical, psychological, and material scars well into adulthood. CSEC victims are faceless, nameless, and displaced from society; victims of commercial sexual exploitation are anonymous to the public's concern and often left forgotten.

References

Adelson, W. J. (2008). Child prostitute or victim of trafficking? *University of St Thomas Law Journal, 6*, 96–128.

Aggravated Sexual Abuse of Children. 18 USC § 2421.

Arlacchi, P. (2000). Against all the godfathers: The revolt of the decent people. The World Against Crime, Special Issue of Giornale di Silica

Aronowitz, A. (2001). Smuggling and trafficking in human beings: The phenomenon, the markets that drive it and the organizations that promote it. *European Journal on Criminal Policy and Research, 9*, 163–195.

Berkman, E. T. (1996). Responses to the international child sex tourism trade. *Boston College International Comparative Law Review, 19*, 397–422.

Bertone, A. M. (2000). Sexual trafficking in women: International policy economy and the politics of sex. *Gender Issues, 18*, 4–22.

Blundell, B., Sherry, M., Burke, A., & Sowerbutts, S. (2002). Child Pornography and the Internet: Accessibility and policing. *Australian Police Journal, 56*(1), 59–65.

Bolling, M., & Harper, E. (2007). *The commercial sexual exploitation of children* [white paper, electronic version]. Georgia State University Center for School Safety, School Climate and Classroom Management website: http://education.gsu.edu/schoolsafety/

Bourke, M. L., & Hernandez, A. E. (2009). The 'butner study' redux: A report of the incidence of hands-on child victimization by child pornography offenders. *Journal of Family Violence, 24*, 183–191.

Boxill, N., & Richardson, D. (2007). Ending sex trafficking of children in Atlanta. *Affilia, 22*, 138–149.

Brannigan, A., & Van Brunschot, E. G. (1997). Youthful prostitution and child sexual trauma. *International Journal of Law and Psychiatry, 20*, 337–354.

Bump, M. N. (2009). Treat the children well: Shortcomings in the U.S'. effort to protect child trafficking victims. *Notre Dame Journal of Law, Ethics & Public Policy, 23*, 73–107.

Bump, M. N., & Duncan, J. (2003). Conference on identifying and serving child victims of trafficking. *International Migration, 41*, 201–218.

Bump, M., Duncan, J., Gozdziak, E., & Macdonnell, M. (2005). Second conference on identifying and serving child victims of trafficking. *International Migration, 43*, 343–363.

Bureau of International Labor, U.S. Department of Labor. (1994). *By the sweat and toil of children: The use of child labor in American imports, 2.* Available at: http://www.dol.gov/ilab/media/reports/iclp/sweat/sweat.pdf

Burke, M. C. (2012). Human trafficking: An overview for law enforcement. *Law Enforcement Executive Forum: Human Trafficking, 12*, 1–178.

Burke, A., Sowerbutts, S., Blundell, B., & Sherry, M. (2002). Child pornography and the Internet: Policing and treatment issues. *Psychiatry, Psychology & Law, 9*, 79–84.

Calder, M. (2004). *Child sexual abuse and the internet: Tackling the new frontier.* Lyme Regis: Russell House Publishing.

Candappa, M. (2003). *Scoping exercise on trafficking of children and young people to and through the UK.* Report to the Save the Children, UK (unpublished).

Chase, E., & Statham, J. (2004). The commercial sexual exploitation of children and young people: An overview of key literature and data. Thomas Coram Research Unit Institute of Education, University of London.

Chase, E., & Statham, J. (2005). Commercial and sexual exploitation of children and young people in the UK: A review. *Child Abuse Review, 14*, 4–25.

Child Pornography. 18 U.S.C. § 2256.

Child Trafficking, Traveling, and Luring for Participation in Illegal Sexual Activity. 18 U.S.C. § 2423(a)(b).

Dalla, R. L. (2000). Exposing the "pretty woman" myth: A qualitative examination of the lives of female streetwalking prostitutes. *The Journal of Sex Research, 37*, 344–353.

De Fabrique, N., Romano, S. J., Vecchi, G. M., & Van Hasselt, V. B. (2007). Understanding stockholm syndrome. *FBI Law Enforcement Bulletin, 76*, 10–15.

Donovan, K. (1991). Hidden from view. An explanation of the little-known world of young male prostitutes in Great Britain and Europe. Home Office and West Midlands Police.

Duffin, T. (2004). Transforming the response to young people exploited through prostitution. In M. Melrose & D. Barrett (Eds.), *Anchors in floating lives: Models of practice with young people sexually exploited through prostitution (provisional title).* Lyme Regis: Russell House Publishing.

Esposito, L. (1998). Regulating the internet: The new battle against child pornography. *Case Western Reserve Journal of International Law, 30*, 541–565.

Estes, R. J. (2001). *The sexual exploitation of children: A working guide to the empirical literature.* University of Pennsylvania, School of Social Work. Philadelphia. PA.

Estes, R. J., & Weiner, N. A. (2001). *The commercial sexual exploitation of children in the U.S., Canada and Mexico.* University of Pennsylvania School of Social Work, Philadelphia.

Finkelhor, D. (1994). Current information on the scope and nature of child sexual abuse. *Future of Children, 4*, 31–53.

Finkelhor, D., & Ormrod, R. (2004). Prostitution of juveniles: Patterns from NIBRS. *OJJDP Juvenile Justice Bulletin*, 1–11.

First World Congress against Commercial Sexual Exploitation of Children. (1996). *Declaration and Agenda for Action.* Available at: http://www.csecworldcongress.org/PDF/en/Stockholm/Outome_documents/Stockholm%20Declaration%201996_EN.pdf

Fong, R., & Berger Cardoso, J. (2010). Child human trafficking victims: Challenges for the child welfare system. *Evaluation and Program Planning, 33*, 311–316.

Forde, P., & Patterson, A. (1998). Pedophile internet activity. *Trends & Issues in Crime & Criminal Justice, 97*. Canberra: Australian Institute of Criminology. Available at: www.aic.gove.au/publications/tandi/ti97.pdf

Fraley, A. (2012). Child sex tourism legislation under the PROTECT act: Does it really protect? *St. John's Law Review, 79*(7), 445–483.

Gillen, A. (2003). Race to save new victims of child porn. *The Guardian, 4*, 1–2.

Goddard, V., & White, B. (1982). Child workers and capitalist development: An introductory note and bibliography. *Development and Change, 13*, 465–477.

Graham, W. R. (2000). Uncovering and eliminating child pornography rings on the internet: Issues regarding and avenues facilitating law enforcements access to 'wonderland'. *Law Review of Michigan State University, 2*, 457–484.

Halter, S. (2010). Factors that influence police conceptualizations of girls involved in prostitution in six U.S. cities: Child sexual exploitation victims or delinquents? *Child Maltreatment, 15*, 152–160.

References

Hanna, C. (2002). Somebody's daughter: The domestic trafficking of girls for the commercial sex industry and the power of love. *William & Mary Journal of Women and the Law, 9*, 1–29.

Hanson, R. K., & Bussiere, M. T. (1998). Predicting relapse: A metaanalysis of sexual offender recidivism studies. *Journal of Consulting and Clinical Psychology, 66*, 348–363.

Healy, M. A. (1996). Child pornography: An international perspective: A working document for the World Congress against commercial sexual exploitation of children, Stockholm, Sweden, August 27–31, 1996.

Hernandez, A. (2000). *Self-reported contact sexual offenses by participants in the federal bureau of prisons' sex offender treatment program: implications for internet sex offenders.* Paper presented at the 19th Annual Research and Treatment Conference of the Association for the Treatment of Sexual Abusers, San Diego.

Hodge, D. R., & Lietz, C. A. (2007). The international sexual trafficking of women and children. *Journal of Women and Social Work, 22*, 163–174.

Hughes, D. M. (2008). Combating sex trafficking: A perpetrator-focused approach. *University of St. Thomas Law Journal, 6*, 28–53.

Hughes, D. M. (2000). The 'Natasha' trade: The transnational shadow market of trafficking in women. *Journal of International Affairs, 53*(2), 625–651.

Hughes, D. M. (1999). Pimps and predators on the internet: Globalizing the sexual exploitation of women and children. University of Rhode Island, Women's Studies Program, Available at: University of Rhode Island, Women's Studies Program, Available at: http://www.prostitutionetsociete.fr/IMG/pdf/2004huguesbestpracticestoadressdemandside.pdf

Hughes, D. M., Carlson, E. M., & Carlson, O. M. (2004). *Best practices to address the demand side of sex trafficking.* University of Rhode Island, Women's Studies Program, Available at: http://www.prostitutionetsociete.fr/IMG/pdf/2004huguesbestpracticestoadressdemandside.pdf

Kapstein, E. B. (2003). The baby trade. *Foreign Affairs, 82*, 115–125.

Kendall, V. M., & Funk, T. M. (2012). *Child exploitation and trafficking: Examining the global challenges and U.S. responses.* Lanham: Rowman & Littlefield Publisher Inc.

Kern, C. M. (2000). Child labor: The international law and corporate impact. *Syracuse Journal of International Law & Commerce, 27*, 177–198.

Krone, T. (2004). A typology of online child pornography offending. *Trends & Issues in Crime and Criminal Justice, 279*. Canberra: Australian Institute of Criminology. Available at: www.aic.gov.au/publications/tandi2/tandi279.pdf

Lanning, K. V. (2001). *Child molesters: A behavioral analysis* [Monograph]. Arlington: National Center for Missing and Exploited Children.

Lanning, K. V. (2008). Cyber "pedophiles": A behavioral perspective [section IV]. In R. R. Hazelwood & A. W. Burgess (Eds.), *Practical aspects of rape investigation: A multidisciplinary approach* (Vol. 4, pp. 71–87). NY: CRC Press.

Li, V. F. (1995). Child sex tourism to Thailand: The role of the U.S. as a consumer country. *Pacific Rim Law & Policy Association, 4*, 505–542.

Lim, L. L. (1998). *Child prostitution* (pp. 170–205). Geneva, Switzerland: International Labour Office.

McKegany, N., & Bloor, M. (1990). A risky business. *Community Care, 5*, 301.

Medaris, M., & Girouard, C. (2002). Protecting children in cyberspace: The ICAC Task Force Program. U.S. Department of Justice, pp. 1–8.

Melrose, M., Barnett, D., & Brodie, I. (1999). *One way street? Retrospectives on childhood prostitution.* The Children's Society and University of London.

Mikhail, S. L. (2002). Child marriage and child prostitution: Two forms of sexual exploitation. *Gender and Development, 10*, 43–49.

Mitchell, K. J., Jones, L. M., Finkelhor, D., & Wolak, J. (2011). Internet-facilitated commercial sexual exploitation of children: Findings from a nationally representative sample of law enforcement agencies in the U.S. *Sex Abuse, 23*, 43–71.

Moran, M. (1993). Ending exploitative child labor practices. *Pace International Law Review, 5*, 287–312.

Mostyn, M. (2000). The need for regulating anonymous remailers. *International Review of Law, Computers & Technology, 14*, 79–88.

Palmer, T. (2001) *No son of mine! Children abused through prostitution*. Barkingside: Barnardo's.

Palmer, T. & Stacey, L. (2002). *Stolen childhood: Barnardo's work with children abused through prostitution*. New York: Barnardo's.

Pearce, J. (2003). *It's someone taking a part of you: A study of young women and sexual exploitation*. London: National Children's Bureau.

Petrunov, G. (2011). Managing money acquired from human trafficking: Case study of sex trafficking from Bulgaria to Western Europe. *Trends in Organized Crime, 14*, 165–183.

Phoenix, J. (2002). In the name of protection: Youth prostitution policy reforms in England and Wales. *Critical Social Policy, 22*, 353–375.

Rahman, M. A. (2011). Human trafficking in the era of globalization: The case of Trafficking in the global market economy. *Transcience Journal, 2*, 54–71.

Robinson, L. N. (1997). The globalization of female child prostitution: A call for reintegration and recovery measures via article 39 of the United Nations Convention on the right s of the child. *Indiana Journal of Global Legal Studies, 5*, 239–261.

Sarrica, F. (2009). *Trafficking in persons: Analysis on Europe. United Nations office on drugs and crime*. Available at: http://www.unodc.org/documents/human-trafficking/Trafficking_in_Persons_in_Europe_09.pdf

Scarpa, S. (2006). Child trafficking: International instruments to protect the most vulnerable victims. *Family Court Review, 44*, 429–447.

Schauer, E. J., & Wheaton, E. M. (2006). Sex trafficking into the U.S.: A literature review. *Criminal Justice Review, 31*, 146–169.

Schneider, J. P. (2000). Effects of cybersex addiction on the family: Results of a survey. In A. Cooper (Ed.), *Cybersex: The dark side of the force*. New York: Brunner/Mazel.

Schwartz, M. F., & Southern, S. (2000). Compulsive cybersex. In A. Cooper (Ed.), *Cybersex: The dark side of the force*. New York: Brunner/Mazel.

Seto, M., Cantor, J., & Blanchard, R. (2006). Child pornography offenses are a valid diagnostic indicator of pedophilia. *Journal of Abnormal Psychology, 115*, 610–615.

Seto, M. C., Reeves, L., & Jung, S. (2010). Explanations given by child pornography offenders for their crimes. *Journal of Sexual Aggression, 16*, 169–180.

Smolin, D. M. (2006). Child laundering: How the intercountry adoption system legitimizes and incentivizes the practices of buying, trafficking, kidnapping, and stealing children. *The Wayne Law Review, 52*, 112–200.

Smolin, D. M. (2007). Child laundering as exploitation: Applying anti-trafficking norms to intercountry adoption under the coming Hague Regime. *Vermont Law Review, 32*, 1–56.

Spangenberg, M. (2001). *Prostituted youth in New York city: An overview*. New York: End Child Prostitution and Trafficking.

Spidel, A., Greaves, C., Cooper, B. S., Herve, H., Hare, R. D., & Yuille, J. C. (2006). The psychopath as pimp. *The Canadian Journal of Police & Security Services, 4*, 193–199.

Steinman, K. J. (2002). Sex tourism and the child: Latin America's and the U.S'. failure to prosecute sex tourists. *Hastings women's law journal, 13*, 53–76.

Svensson, N. L. (2006). Extraterritorial accountability: An assessment of the effectiveness of child sex tourism laws. *Loyola of Los Angeles International and Comparative Law Review, 28*, 641.

Taylor, M., & Quayle, E. (2003). *Child pornography: An internet crime*. New York: Brunner-Routledge.

Taylor-Browne, J., Broadfoot, F., Broadhead, L., Downie, A., & McKetty-Campbell, M. (2002). *More than one chance: Young people involved in prostitution speak out London*. London: End Child Prostitution and.

The Mann Act (1910), 36 Stats, Vol. I, p. 825.

Thomas, F., & Mathews, L. (2006). *Who are the child sex tourists in Cambodia?* Child Wise. Available at: www.ChildWise.net

References

Thornburg, D., & Lin, H. (2002). *Youth, pornography and the internet*. Washington D.C.: National Academy Press.

Todres, J. (1999). Prosecuting sex tour operators in U.S. courts in an effort to reduce the sexual exploitation of children globally. B.U. *Public Interest Law Journal, 9*, 1–23.

UN General Assembly. (2000). *Convention against transnational organized crime and the protocols* thereto. United Nations, Treaty Series, 1577, p. 42. Available at: http://www.unodc.org/documents/treaties/UNTOC/Publications/TOC%20Convention/TOCebook-e.pdf.html

U.S. Department of Justice Child Exploitation and Obscenity Section. (2011). *Child sexual trafficking*. Available at: http://www.justice.gov/criminal/ceos/sextour.html

U.S. Department of Justice. (2007). Commercial Sexual Exploitation of Children: What Do We Know and What Do We Do About It? Human Trafficking: Data and Documents. Paper 6. http://digitalcommons.unl.edu/humtraffdata/6

U.S. Department of State. (2004). Trafficking in persons report, 4th ed.

Vayrynen, R. (2003). *Illegal immigration, human trafficking, and organized crime*. United Nations University World Institute for development Econocomics Research. Available at: http://www.wider.unu.edu/publications/working-papers/discussion-papers/2003/en_GB/dp2003-072/_files/78091733799863273/default/dp2003-072.pdf

Walker-Rodriguez, A., & Hill, R. (2011). Human sex trafficking. *FBI Law Enforcement Bulletin, 80*, 1–9.

Walters, J., & Davis, P. H. (2011). Human trafficking, sex tourism, and child exploitation on the southern border. *Journal of Applied Research on Children: Informing Policy for Children at Risk, 2*, 1–17.

Wasserman, A. J. (1998). Virtual.child.porn.com: Defending the constitutionality of the criminalization of computer-generated child pornography by the child pornography prevention act of 1996: A reply to Professor Burke and other critics. *Harvard J Legislation, 35*, 245

Webb, L., Craissati, J., & Keen, S. (2007). Characteristics of internet child pornography offenders: A comparison with child molesters. *Sex Abuse: A Journal of Research and Treatment, 19*, 449–465.

William Wilberforce Trafficking Victims Protection Reauthorization Act of 2008 [U.S. of America], Public Law 110–457, 23 December 2008. Available at: http://www.unhcr.org/refworld/docid/49805ae72.html

Williams, L. M., & Frederick, M. E. (2009). *Pathways into and out of commercial sexual victimization of children: Understanding and responding to sexually exploited teens*. Lowell: University of Massachusetts.

Willis, B. M., & Levy, B. S. (2002). Child prostitution: Global health burden, research needs, and interventions. *The Lancet, 359*, 1417–1422.

Wolak, J., Finkelhor, D., & Mitchell, K. J. (2005). *Child pornography possessors arrested in Internet-related crimes: Findings from the National Juvenile Online Victimization Study* (NCMEC 06–05–023). Alexandria, VA: National Center for Missing & Exploited Children.

Wonders, N. A., & Michalowski, R. (2001). Bodies, borders, and sex tourism in a globalized world: A tale of two cities—Amsterdam and Havana. *Social Problems, 48*, 545–571.

Wyler, L. S., & Siskin, A. (2010). *Trafficking in persons: U.S. policy and issues for congress*. CRS Report for Congress. Available at: http://fpc.state.gov/documents/organization/139278.pdf